with Local Tips
*The author's special recommendations are
highlighted in yellow throughout this guide*

There are five symbols to help you find your way around this guide:

Marco Polo's top recommendations – the best in each category

sites with a scenic view

places where the local people meet

places where young people get together

(100/A1)
pages and coordinates for the Road Atlas of Menorca
(U/A1) *coordinates for City Maps of Mahón and Ciutadella*
inside back cover
(O) *area not covered by the City Maps*

*This guide was written by Jörg Dörpinghaus. An advertising expert he has
lived since 1985 in the Balearic Islands where he is well known as an author
of German language publications and in the sphere of environmental issues.*

MARCO ✜ POLO

Travel guides and language guides in this series:

Alaska • Algarve • Amsterdam • Australia/Sydney • Bahamas • Barbados
Barcelona • Berlin • Brittany • Brussels • California • Canada • Channel
Islands • Chicago and the Great Lakes • Costa Brava/Barcelona • Costa del
Sol/Granada • Côte d'Azur • Crete • Cuba • Cyprus • Dominican Republic
Eastern Canada • Eastern USA • Egypt • Florence • Florida • Gran Canaria • Greek
Islands/Aegean • Hong Kong • Ibiza/Formentera • Ireland • Israel • Istanbul
Lanzarote • London • Los Angeles • Madeira • Mallorca • Malta • Mexico • Minorca
New York • New Zealand • Normandy • Norway • Paris • Portugal • Prague
Rhodes • Rocky Mountains • Rome • San Francisco • Scotland • South Africa
Southwestern USA • Tenerife • Thailand • Turkish Coast • Tuscany
USA: New England • USA: Southern States • Venice • Washington D.C.
Western Canada • Western USA

French • German • Italian • Spanish

*Marco Polo would be very interested to hear your
comments and suggestions. Please write to:*

North America:
Marco Polo North America
70 Bloor Street East
Oshawa, Ontario, Canada
(B) 905-436-2525

United Kingdom:
GeoCenter International Ltd
The Viables Centre
Harrow Way
Basingstoke, Hants RG22 4BJ

Cover photograph: Cala Macarelleta (Huber: R. Schmid)
Photos: G. Amberg (4, 18, 20, 37); Author (24); O. Baumli (48, 78); H. Hartmann (90); HB Verlag,
Hamburg (7, 26, 28, 39, 52, 57, 64); Lade: Ott (72), Wrba (77); Mauritius: AGE Kat. (83),
Hubatka (99), Mehlig (32, 58), Waldkirch (31, 50), World P./Holt (62);
K. Thiele (10, 47, 55); Timmermann (14, 23, 66)

1st edition 2000
© Mairs Geographischer Verlag, Ostfildern, Germany
Translator: Brenda Ferris
English edition 2000: Margaret Court
Editorial director: Ferdinand Ranft
Chief editor: Marion Zorn
Cartography for the Road Atlas: ©Mairs Geographischer Verlag
Design and layout: Thienhaus/Wippermann
Printed in Germany

CONTENTS

Discover Menorca!

Can holidays spell ruin?
A natural paradise tries to remain unspoilt

On two occasions the Balearic Government – which covers all the islands and is based on Menorca's big sister, neighbouring Mallorca – has intervened with a heavy hand in the choice of the title photo for Menorca's main brochure. In 1983 the *Govern Balear* came up with a picture of Formentera instead of one of the enchanting Menorcan bays. And then in the 1994 edition the northernmost of the Balearic islands was again adorned with borrowed plumes. This time the publicity handout for Menorca plugged Cala Pí in Mallorca on its first page. The mistaken intervention was not only embarrassing, it was, more importantly, entirely unnecessary: some of the most beautiful and – what is probably nowadays almost more significant – "virginal" idyllic coves and sheltered bays for swimming and relaxing are precisely to be found on the smaller of the two *Gymnesiae*, as Mallorca and Menorca were known in Classical times. The turquoise-blue waves lapping the Cala Macarella, the pine groves, gently swaying in the sea breezes, of the Cala En Turqueta,

Cala Rafalet — the rugged romantic cove close to Mahón

the shell-shaped beach of d'en Castell, the centuries-old cave dwellings in the Cales Coves – the beauty of all of these has inspired Menorca's poets just as much as they have enthused the more prosaically minded holidaymaker.

The paradox is that it is precisely these impressive natural beauties that could prove the island's future undoing. In times when such an unspoilt and untamed natural world is becoming an ever rarer commodity, these very attributes are helping to boost its market value. So, no doubt about it, Menorca is "in". Since the entire island was quite recently declared a *Reserva de la Biosfera*, a "Biosphere Reserve", by the Unesco "Mankind and Biosphere" committee, tourism-based business has been booming as never before. Thus in the first six months of 1995 passenger numbers for international flights topped the 600,000 limit, a barrier that hitherto had seemed insurmountable. In the same period the figure for holidaymakers was up by 14 per cent in comparison with 1994. The GOB, the most active environmental protection organization in the Balearics, and the largest private body of its kind in Spain by any standards, is consequently setting the alarm bells ringing. The environmentalists warn that applications already filed for building permits are likely to result in a doubling of the existing hotel capacity, with Menorca then facing the threat of being strangled by its own success.

The government is also well aware of the problem and has enacted counter-measures to ensure that Nature remains unspoilt. Not for nothing are the waters around the Balearics amongst the cleanest in the Mediterranean. Taking as their slogan that no single drop of untreated sewage should be allowed to get into the sea, the authorities have been building sewage plants since the 1970s. Today Menorca has a purification rate of no less than 95 per cent. That is far above the rest of Spain, and, for that matter, the EU average, which has barely attained 82 per cent. In a second phase of constructing treatment works the existing plant is now being equipped with a third filtration stage. Acting on the new slogan, that no single drop of used water should get into the sea, from now on treated waste water is being recycled, not only for use in farming and for livestock, but also for watering parks and green spaces, and the sludge is being processed in a composting plant, using German know-how.

Since 1991/92, under revolutionary environmental-protection legislation, parts of the Balearics – amounting to 39.75 per cent of their total surface – have been designated as nature conservation areas. In these so-called *espacios naturales* (natural

spaces) there is a ban on unrestricted building, and in areas with even stricter protection the ban actually extends to the use of cars. On Menorca itself 42.67 per cent of the island comes under this form of conservation.

Soothing green shade is mainly provided by the larger wooded areas. Around 40 per cent of the island is wooded, chiefly with parasol and Aleppo pines, and large tracts of woodland surround the townships of Es Mercadal (6500 ha), Ciutadella (2500 ha), and Ferreríes (1600 ha). But Menorca also has quite a lot to offer in terms of its many varieties of flora. Thus in the water-worn gullies, the *barrancs*, there are over 200 different varieties of plants, 25 of which are only found on Menorca. Several kinds of fauna are also closely bound up with this island habitat. The *cavalls*, for example, belong to a special race of horses that is only found here, and the island has even been declared a gene-bank for ten species of fauna and four varieties of flora. These specially protected species include the local milch cows, but also rarer birds such as kites, eagles and falcons, the Egyptian vulture, and sea turtles that are threatened with extinction.

As leading island geographer Paul Fallot wryly observed, Menorca, as it appears on the map, is not unlike a giant broad bean. And it also reminds him of a kidney-shaped table, flat, with a gently curving hollow towards the south and a rugged hump that defies the biting north winds. In fact the island does have two sides that are basically different. The Tramuntana in the north, with "fjords" reaching deep into the interior, bizarre rock formations and an irregular coastline dotted with natural harbours, is in strong contrast to the Migjorn in the south with its more compact coast, with small coves, wooded valleys and the *barrancs* already mentioned. The south also has most of the beaches so consequently this is where the most tourists are to be found. A clear geological dividing line runs from Cala Morell in the west to Mahón in the southeast. This is where the most ancient landmass in the Balearics – dark slatey rock – comes up against the much younger pale limestone that is so typical of the Mediterranean zone.

With a total surface area of 701.84 square kilometres Menorca is one and a half times as large as Ibiza, but only a fifth of the size of Mallorca. From Cap Sa Mola to Cap de Bajolí the island measures 47 kilometres in length, while its width is between 10 and 19 kilometres.

Offshore a chain of 30 or so small islands and even tinier islets skirts the 285.7 km coastline. The most important are Illa de les Bledes, Illa dels Porros, Illa d'en Colom, Illa de l'Aire and the Illas d'Addaia; needless to say no one lives on them any more.

Menorca is separated from its big sister Mallorca by scarcely 75 km at the narrowest point by sea, namely between Cap d'Artrutx and Cap Freu. Barcelona is 241 km away and Africa is only 380 km or so. That probably accounts for the mild average temperature which, in summer, is around 25° centigrade and is still no less than 14° centigrade in winter, with over 2452 hours of sunshine a year; what is not clear, though, is why these average figures are so much less variable than are those for the Spanish mainland and for Mallorca. Another curious feature is that the average temperature in the Tramuntana is 1 to 2 degrees lower than it is in the Migjorn on the south side.

Both ends of the island are also

Bare rock is the abiding image at Cala Morell

as different from one another as the north is from the south side. Uptight, hardworking Mahón in the east, which in earlier times was quite prepared to concede to colonialism, is in sharp contrast to the more rebellious and yet at the same time more conciliatory Ciutadella in the west – Mediterranean charm but without Mediterranean ease of acceptance. There are also signs of clear distinctions between the two in architecture and also in social structure and general attitudes. The competition between both places has been smouldering away for centuries. Even today the true Ciutadellans are reluctant to travel to Mahón to do business or engage in any dealings with the authorities that they cannot get out of. The Mahonese treat this with a certain sense of superiority – those in the capital tend to look upon any pronouncements from the western province somewhat askance, commenting upon them with a reticent but meaningful raising of the left eyebrow. The little town at the other end of the island is nice enough, to be sure – but at the end of the day what they say there makes no difference.

Menorca's roots reach far back into history. People are supposed to have inhabited the island more than 6500 years ago. The oldest traces – imperishable stone buildings, put together without mortar – date back between 4000 and 5000 years. In some areas – such as around Es Migjorn Gran – there are 50 to 60 archaeological sites to the square kilometre. There is a greater density of burial sites here than anywhere else in Europe. Menorca has therefore justifiably earned the title of one "large open air museum", so it is no wonder that Spain's first archaeological publications were penned on the island. Prehistoric caves and settlements, the *coves* and *talaiots*, age-old ritual sites with their stone tables, the *taulas*, the remains of five basilicas and the *navetas*, wreathed in fable and probably Europe's oldest surviving roofed buildings, still await exploration and explanation of the key to their existence.

The Phoenicians, Greeks, Cathaginians and Romans were later to exploit the island's strategic location, then it was seized by the Byzantines and finally brought under Islamic rule by the Moors. It was 1287 before Menorca, apparently at the tail-end of the Christian reconquest of Spain, was wrested from the grasp of the "Unbelievers". For the islanders of that time this was not necessarily a turn for the better, since famine and disease were to follow in the wake of a Christian occupation that was only marginally interested in Menorca.

According to the historian Jaume Sastre, his study of 15th-century documents showed the people to be mainly craftsmen and artisans. At that time most of the population lived in the villages; these in their turn were involved in a brisk trade with the neighbouring island in the south-west, but also with other parts of Europe, especially southern France and Catalonia. These crafts were further encouraged in the 18th century by the English. The island chronicles show that in 1784 there were 21 goldsmiths, descendants of the many jewellers of Jewish origin; they were the forerunners of the present fashion-jewellery manufacturers. The census also attests to 150 shoemakers with over 50 apprentices. Decades later shoemaking was to undergo a severe crisis, but it recovered again following the introduction of modern sewing machines to such an extent that by the end of the 19th century almost 40 per cent of the Menorcans were able to earn their living from producing shoes. Menorca's footwear industry also seems to have got over the crisis in the 1980s without too much damage; this time it was not better machines but exclusive design and excellent workmanship that saved the day. At the turn of the previous century Menorca was already known for its fashion accessories; these included fine silver-mesh evening bags, designed for evenings out at the opera or the theatre – items that can still be found today on stalls in some of the better local markets.

Farm products can also boast a long tradition. Thus in the first half of the 5th century a pastoral letter from Severus, the island's bishop, was singing the praises of the aromatic *caseus* to his flock. Flavourful Menorcan cheese travelled with Christian seafarers on their voyages as an accompaniment to stale ship's biscuit. Nowadays the annual yield of Menorca's 340 dairy farmers produces around 5000 tonnes of cheese, most of which is then industrially processed, melted down, and sold under brand names. Only around 30 per cent is produced by hand in the traditional way and sold individually as *queso artesanal*. Since April 1985 these have been stamped with the *denominación de origen* (designation of origin) which serves as a kind of hallmark.

Fishing is not as important as it used to be. Currently less than 160 boats put out to sea on a daily basis to catch fresh fish and spiny lobster, and this is almost exclusively for local consumption. The largest fishing ports are Mahón, Ciutadella and Fornells.

The best way to spell out the current importance of the service sector is probably to quote a few

---

Instead of Hard Tack: Menorca Cheese

The typical consistency of Menorca cheese (hard and dry), and its square shape (which meant it was practical to stow and easy to store), date back to the days of the windjammer and the sailing frigate. Apart from a few exceptions the method of production is largely industrial (around 70 per cent). Thus they now add modern casein to make the milk coagulate instead of artichokes as they did in the olden days. The cheeses get their characteristic rounded corners from being wrapped in cotton cloths during pressing. The usual weight is from 1 to 4 kilos. The *mahonés* come in three degrees of ripeness: semicurado (buttery, 2 – 5 months old), *curado* (hard, over 5 months old) and *añejo* (dry, more than 10 months old).

A typical Menorcan "finca" in its setting of lush greenery

figures. Out of every hundred Menorcans in employment 7 work in the fields and pastures, 18 in the building trade, 20 in industry and manufacturing. The remaining 55 earn their living – as sales assistants, shopkeepers, waiters or porters – directly or indirectly from the tourist trade. And to top that here is another impressive statistic: in 1995 Menorca airport greeted its 25 millionth air passenger. The island president interrupted his official duties to do the honours, a folk-dance group danced *boleros*, and the top brass from the travel agency immediately threw in an extra fortnight's holiday.

Needless to say, the over 1 million passengers (Spaniards included) who, year on year, jet into Menorca on almost 10,000 flights are not received in such style. Around a quarter of them are here on business, to buy cheese or to sell airbeds, beer and potato crisps. Another group is made up of Cen-

tral Government officials and guest workers from the Spanish mainland who mainly work in tourism but often spend the winter half of the year back in their own country. The remaining 600,000 are flying in to get a tan, enjoy a swim and to relax – in that order, according to a survey. It goes without saying that visitors to Menorca also have motivations and expectations of their holidays that are different from those of tourists visiting the neighbouring islands of Ibiza and Mallorca. Thus what distinguishes the "classic" Menorca enthusiast is a heightened interest in culture and tradition, as well as a greater love of the landscape and its conservation. Visitors of this kind usually also have more purchasing power at their disposal, but whether they are prepared to spend this on just anything is another matter.

This is what Menorcan business people learnt to their cost when they went to the lengths of carrying out a survey following a lean period. According to 64 per cent of the Germans and 41 per cent of the British visitors in the survey the quality of the goods on offer was only fair to middling or even downright bad. Ninety per cent of both nationalities were in agreement on pricing: their unanimous verdict was "too expensive". Bars and restaurants on their own came out better. In 86 per cent of cases they were given a positive rating, and 25 per cent of visitors were actually extremely satisfied. There were also smiling faces among the departing guests: 89 per cent of them definitely wanted to return to Menorca – 57 per cent felt that their holiday expectations had been pretty much fulfilled while 32 per cent were extremely enthusiastic.

Over half these visitors are from the United Kingdom, followed some way behind by Germany and Spain, each with around 15 per cent; the rest are from Austria, the Benelux countries, and Scandinavia. The accommodation on offer was to most people's taste: 194 apartment hotels with 19,099 beds, as compared with a comparatively small number of hotels – 95 of them, with 21,036 bed spaces. As for what is already a booming trend elsewhere in Spain, Menorca tends to be moving more cautiously. Up until 1996 only three farms, with a total of 12 beds, had latched on to *agroturisme* as they call "farm holidays" here. There are only a couple of campsites, and they barely satisfy the demand. Here it is advisable to book; off-site camping can end up in some nasty surprises. As for leisure activities, these are catered for in all kinds of different ways by nine marinas with 840 moorings, a large number of water sports facili-

ties, a nine-hole golf course and at least 30 tennis courts at the various hotels.

And the people themselves, whose home this is, the 65,000 Menorcans? Gentle, good-hearted, hospitable, cosmopolitan, inspired by impeccable morals and love of their motherland (the island!) – this is how Archduke Ludwig Salvator, an expert on the Balearics, characterized the island people a hundred years ago. Since then hardly anything has changed. So far the locals are still hospitable and good-hearted, so far, in magic Menorca, ancient legends still live in close harmony with the most progressive minds in the Balearics. Numbered among them, for example, are Joan Ramis, who was already writing up scientific treatises on the island's history back in 1780, Mateu Orfila, physician, toxicologist and for a time Dean of the Medical Faculty in Paris, Francesc Camps, historian and chronicler of legends and customs, and so the list of Menorca's illustrious offspring goes on. Raised to be ever civilized and freedom-loving, the Menorcans are open-minded and receptive so far as the sciences, fine arts and political and social issues are concerned. That becomes particularly clear at election time; politically, Menorca is less right-wing than any of the other Balearics, and seems to show a certain affinity with Barcelona.

The Menorcans are more worldly-wise and cosmopolitan than the less sophisticated Balearic central government on Mallorca. While in Mallorca they are stretching the limits of the *Plan General de Ordenación de la Oferta Turística* (POOT for short: the plan for sensibly

History at a glance

From about 6500 BC
Migration to Menorca from the mainland, presumably in reed-boats

2000 BC
First traces of settlement, megaliths, construction of the first *navetas*

1300 BC
First evidence of the *talaiot* culture

1000 BC
Construction of the great *talaiot* edifices and walled towns

470 BC
Phoenician influences

205 BC
Hannibal's brother Mago invades Menorca and founds Maó (Mahón) which is named after him

From 123 BC
Roman occupation and downfall of the *talaiot* culture; the last *talaiot* towns were probably inhabited up to around A.D. 100

From 425
Menorca in the hands of the Vandals

From 534
Byzantine Empire period of influence, during which time the basilicas were built on the island

From 903
Moorish occupation; Menorca is attached to the caliphate at Córdoba

1287
Reconquest of Menorca by King Alfonso III of Aragón; the conquered Moors are promised free passage to North Africa but are thrown overboard soon after the transport ships set sail

From 1500
Pirates attack and destroy Mahón (Redbeard, 1535) and Ciutadella (Turks, 1558)

1706–1708
In the War of the Spanish Succession, Menorcan followers of the Habsburg claimant to the Spanish throne, Archduke Charles of Austria (who was to become Holy Roman Emperor Charles VI in 1711), rise up, with Joan Saura at their head, against the threat of Bourbon rule, but are beaten back by Governor Dávila and his French troops; then he in his turn surrenders to English and Dutch troops who land in the Cala d'Alcaufar in 1708

1712
Supported by a secret agreement (before the Treaty of Utrecht) the British take official possession of Menorca for the first time

1756
Capture of the island by French troops under Marshal Richelieu

1763–1802

Menorca is handed back to the British without bloodshed in the Treaty of Paris (1763); French and Spanish troops capture Menorca for Spain (1781), recaptured again by the British (1798); Menorca finally reverts to Spain (1802) under the Treaty of Amiens

1939

Menorca, which in 1931 had declared for the republic and had remained on the side of Franco's opponents throughout the Civil War, falls to the Nationalists

1953

The first charter flight (a British one) reaches the island

1983

The Balearics become a *Comunitat Autónoma*; this also gives them the right to have their own language

1991

The Balearic Parliament enacts an eco-protection law that places over a third of the island under nature conservation

7 October 1993

Unesco proclaims Menorca a *Reserva de la Biosfera*

1995

The island welcomes its 25 millionth air passenger

1998

Menorca is in the throes of an economic boom

restricting the growth of holiday places) as far as they will go – and even beyond in far too many cases unfortunately – Menorca seems to be going down the opposite path. The first official reaction of the Menorcan Hoteliers Assocation was to complain that this "Plan to Regulate Tourist Facilities" was much too lax. According to their members' proposals, they would very much prefer the minimum green space for new hotel complexes to be raised from 60 sq m per guest to 100 sq m. They also wanted the height of hotels to be limited to 7 metres (ground floor plus one storey, as compared with POOT which set the limit at ground floor plus three storeys), and they called for a doubling of the figure in the Plan for the swimming area per guest off a beach. What they are after is not the package tourist but the more affluent, environmentally-aware individual holidaymaker.

All this bodes well for the future. Menorca seems consciously to want to avoid the ruinous follies of its large and small sister-islands in the south-west; it seems to consider its designation as a *Reserva de la Biosfera* not to be just some slick marketing tool, and in fact wants to take it seriously by demonstrating that a sensible measure of tourism need not upset the local culture and social structure, and that it can also live in harmony with unspoilt Nature. Holidays must not spell ruin.

Tanques, taules, talaiots

A cross-section of Menorca's special features, large and small

Arabs

Like almost the whole of Spain Menorca was also at one time occupied by the Moors. From 903 onwards the island belonged to the caliphate at Córdoba and remained under Islamic rule for close on four centuries, until January 1287 when Alfonso III of Aragón recaptured it for Christendom. The Arab population was enslaved, their property was plundered, and their buildings were razed to the ground; nowadays there is hardly an architectural trace of the centuries of Moorish rule to be seen. Where their legacy has been kept alive, though, is in the form of the place names; the prefix *bini* denotes property "of the son of …", the words *rafál* and *cúdia* refer to a house, a cabin or a place "on a hill".

Barrancs

Barrancs – *barrancos* in Spanish – are water-worn gullies that the rain has carved out of the soft limestone over the centuries. On Menorca, protected from the north wind by cliffs that are 20 – 40 metres high, some of these

The Torellonet Vell "talaiot"

naturally sheltered spots became the focus for settlement in earlier times. This is where the most fertile fields are to be found, and some of the richest biotopes (up to 200 floral varieties). The southern side of Menorca, which is considerably younger in geological terms, has 36 *barrancs*, and many of the lovely bays on the south coast are extensions of these. Those that are definitely worth seeing are the Barranc d'Algendar between Ferreríes and Cala Galdana, the Barranc de Trebalùger further east, and the *barrancs* of Son Bou, Es Bec and Son Boter.

Biosphere Reserve

On 7 October 1993 a Unesco Committee ("Mankind and Biosphere") officially approved Menorca's application to be known as *Reserva de la Biosfera*. The application was grounded in a study in the minutest detail of the environment and the island's culture, society, ecology, agriculture and tourism. For one of the main prerequisites for the Unesco rating is not just that the natural environment is intact but there also has to be evidence to show that Man is quite capable of living in that environment without endangering it or even destroying it. *Reserva de la Biosfera* is not some kind of medal that the Menorcans can sport on their chests to show just how proud they are and always will be of their country. It is in fact a dynamic process in which the island must invest year on year so that economy and ecology – which ultimately boils down to tourism and the environment – can peaceably coexist side by side.

The British

The British have captured and occupied Menorca three times in the course of its history. The first was during the War of the Spanish Succession. In 1706 Joan Saura took the side of Charles, the Austrian Archduke, and managed to win over most of the island's communities to his cause. The acting governor, Diego Dávila, barricaded himself in the fortress of San Felipe, and with French support crushed the rebellion in 1707. When English and Dutch troops landed in the Cala d'Alcaufar in the autumn of the following year, the Governor surrendered virtually without a fight. Thus began 48 years of British rule. After the French captured the island in 1756 the British got it back under the Peace of Paris in 1763. During the next 19 years under British sovereignty parts of the San Felipe fortress were blown up and the coastal garrison of Georgetown (now Es Castell) was founded. In 1782 the island was recaptured again, this time by French and Spanish troops, only for them to be supplanted 16 years later following a fresh onslaught by the British, who came back in 1798, this time landing on the north coast. This last period of English rule was for only four years then, in 1802, the Peace of Amiens finally brought the island under the Spanish flag again. Taken as a whole, those nigh on a hundred years of British rule have clearly left their mark on Menorca.

Consell Insular

Policy for the whole of the Balearics is formulated in Mallorca. This is the seat of the *Govern Balear* which is responsible, amongst other things, for matters that affect the other islands such as the power supply and general development control. Each island also has its own local government, the *Consell Insular* (island council). Menorca's *Consell* has long had a reputation for being closer to the Catalan *Generalitat*, the autonomous government of Catalonia, than to the Balearic Government in Palma.

The French

From 1756 Maréchal Armand de Vignerot du Plessis, Duc de Richelieu, and a nephew of Cardinal Richelieu, presided over a brief French interlude for Menorca which, although it only lasted for seven years, was none the less historic for all that. Thus, for example, mayonnaise, that worldwide best seller, is said to have partly been the inspiration of the witty marshall himself; the town of Sant Lluís had the French Governor, Count Lannion, as its founding father; and those who enjoy walking have the French to thank for the *Camí de Cavalls*, certainly the longest path on the island but also, in places, a particularly beautiful one. This "horse road" originally extended along the whole of the coastline to allow for the rapid deployment of the French troops. Nowadays it is ideal for long walks wherever the owner of the land in question allows access.

GOB

This abbreviation stands for *Grup Balear de Ornitolojia i Defensa de la Naturalesa*, a private association which began on Mallorca as a society for the protection of birds and now has over 5000 members throughout the Balearics. The objective of protecting the environment was added some time after it was founded. The GOB is one of Spain's largest and most influential private environmentalist organizations. Birdwatchers and nature conservationists are welcome to make contact with: *GOB Menorca, Camí d'es Castell, 138, 1st Floor, Maó, Tel. 971 35 07 62.* There is someone in the office on weekdays from 9 am to 2.30 pm.

Matanzas

This is what they call the traditional days in late autumn when family pigs are slaughtered, an event on many farms that involves not just the whole family but friends and relations as well. Hence in October and November fresh home-made sausages, such as *sobrasada* (pork and red peppers) and *butifarrón* (spicy blood sausage), are particularly cheap.

Menorquí

Menorquí, Menorcan, is among the oldest of the dialects still in use of *catalá*, Catalan, one of the nine languages of Roman origin introduced into the Balearics by King Alfonso III of Aragón in 1287. In addition all the occupying powers, Roman and Arabic, French and English, left traces of their language behind them. The English words and phrases in common parlance are particularly noticeable. Thus you close the *vindou* (window), have *bifi* (beef, meat) for lunch, and it will be served on a *tibord* (tray, i.e. tea-board), or you have a quick drink, *ha fet un trinqui* (drink). *Catalá* – or rather its local version – has been an official language on the Balearics since February 1983, and is very popular among the younger generation after so many years of the suppression of all regional languages by the Franco dictatorship. Nowadays

---

In the spirit of Marco Polo

Marco Polo was the first true world traveller. He travelled with peaceful intentions forging links between the East and the West. His aim was to discover the world and explore different cultures and environments without changing or disrupting them. He is an excellent role model for the travellers of today and the future. Wherever we travel we should show respect for other peoples and the natural world.

place names and some road signs almost invariably give the Catalan version. Besides *menorquí* people also speak *castellano*, Castilian, i.e. standard Spanish, and often English as well.

Nature conservation

On 30 January 1991 environmental protection legislation was enacted covering the whole of the Balearics, and, following amendment, this bill became law on 23 December 1992. Since then 42.67 per cent of Menorca's surface area enjoys conservation status to a greater or lesser degree (the European average for this kind of protected area is around 7 per cent). The largest conservation areas include the coastline (apart from around Ciutadella and the district south of Mahón), broad swathes of the Tramuntana, the northern half of the island, but also large parts in

the area around Alaior, Cales Coves, and Es Migjorn Gran.

Navetas

The small elongated "pyramids" in the west of Menorca are called *navetas* in Spanish and *naus* in Menorquí because they look like upturned boats. They stem from the Bronze Age (around 2000 B.C.) and served as burial chambers. The oldest – and one of the oldest roofed buildings in Europe overall – is the Nau d'es Tudons, about 4 km from Ciutadella.

Richard Kane

This is a name you are likely to come across quite often on a trip to Menorca. Richard Kane became Governor in 1722, 14 years after the British first occupied the island. Because the citizens of Ciutadella were particularly hostile to the conqueror, Kane, without more ado,

The Albufera lagoon lies at the heart of the Es Grau nature reserve

made Mahón, the town in the east, the seat of administration and the island's capital. Rights and tenure were extensively respected; the changes that the new Governor proposed were more of a practical nature. Thus, for example, he saw to it that the *Camí d'en Kane* – the Kane road, between Mahón and Ciutadella – was paved with a hard surface, he curbed the power of the Spanish Inquisition, and introduced new useful plants, such as apples, and new breeds of livestock – which would also have made him responsible for establishing Menorca's dairy farming. While the clergy and the nobility retired to sulk in Ciutadella the new Governor gained the respect of the country people, something that was never vouchsafed to his successors, Anstruther, Wynyard and Murray.

Talaiots

These prehistoric edifices, which are also to be found on other islands in the Balearics, date back to the 14th–8th century B.C. It was previously supposed that the *talaiots* – which are often constructed out of large rough-hewn blocks of stone and invariably put together without any mortar – were some kind of dwelling, but more recent research indicates that they could have been used for religious or ceremonial purposes. Thus the dimensions and alignment of many *talaiots* seem particularly subject to their own set of laws, and these are currently being investigated.

Tanques

This is what Menorcans call the fields that are surrounded by drystone walls (built without mortar) and usually closed off by a gate. The total length of all the natural stone walls of this kind on the island is supposed to amount to 15,000 kilometres.

Taules

In the island mythology the "tables" were used as furniture by a defunct race of giants. Early island archaeologists considered the actual *taula* – a massive T-shape composed of a stone slab at least 2 to 3 metre high and topped by another, horizontal, stone – was where bloodthirsty Celtic druids carried out human sacrifice. What is more likely is that the *taules* themselves represented a god, possibly, say, a bull. The central stone T is almost always surrounded by a monolithic stone circle. The whole precinct, where an eternal flame burnt and animals were sacrificed, was undoubtedly some kind of temple.

Wildlife

A few species from the animal kingdom are either endemic to Menorca or found here in particularly large numbers. These include the rather ugly little white Egyptian vulture, the *moixeta (Neophron percnopterus)*, which lives mostly on the north coast and, unlike the rest of its kind, is resident and does not migrate south in the winter. Then there is the red kite (*milano real*) which mainly nests on the cliffs by the coast and in tall treetops in the larger woods, and, finally, the short-legged Balearic shrew (*Crocidura suaveolem balearica*) which is extremely shy and lives in shady places and in wall crevices.

Set the table from field and sea

Good plain, honest, peasant fare – authentic Menorcan cuisine is back in favour again

Bon profit! Even though the some of the prices for a *caldereta* may indicate to the contrary, the ringing Menorcan table greeting does not represent the manager, gleefully rubbing his hands as he presents the bill, but is simply the local way of saying "enjoy your meal". Around 370 restaurants, with seating for over 22,500, cater for the creature comforts of their diners on Menorca. Since 1993 the Balearic Government has operated a quality grading – fairly superficial and chiefly concerned with cleanliness, fittings, and number of places – for restaurants (with forks as symbols), bars (goblets), and cafeterias (cups). One symbol is the most modest quality category, and three the top rating.

Just on a third of Menorca's eating places are only there for the holidays and close down at the end of the season. Their standard fare is likely to be an "international menu" that may or may not be particularly good, and probably consists of, say, *beefsteak,*

Mahón's Claustre del Carme: now a covered market

chicken, hamburgers, and occasionally fish, mostly with a generous helping of chips and some salad. Once you have sampled it, you will know just what to expect wherever you go, and may then be curious, perhaps, to find out what else they are cooking up in the local *greixoneras* and *ollas* (earthenware dishes and pots). This is well worth a try, no doubt about it. Menorcan cuisine is good plain fare, tasty, and in all probability high in calories. Cultures go into this melting pot that in history remained impossible to combine. Arabic and Catalan basic recipes get a pragmatic British touch or are enhanced with a fine French flair. What they eat is what they get from the fields and the sea: typical vegetables like tomatoes, artichokes, peas, beans, onions, potatoes, carrots, and cabbages, plus game, lamb, veal, pork, and plenty of fresh fish.

The *caldereta* represents the very best of Menorcan haute cuisine: spiny lobster in a subtle vegetable stew (onions, two cloves of garlic, tomatoes, leeks, seasoned with some parsley and two tablespoonfuls of brandy). It costs around Ptas 6000 per portion: for that you can ask for a live lobster and have it cooked there and then for your delectation. A typical main course menu will include other Anglo-French specialities such as *perdiu amb col* (guinea fowl on cabbage leaves), *albergínies al forn* (baked aubergines) or *olla de mongetes* (bean stew) as well as ancient Moorish recipes. Very good seafood, mostly straight from the sea, also features among the dishes on offer: these include *arrós amb dàtils* ("sea-dates", a kind of shellfish on rice) and *calamar farcit* (stuffed squid), or rather more surprising combinations like *moll salsa de fetge* (sea barbel with liver sauce). What is called *sopas* on neighbouring Mallorca can be found here in the guise of *oli-i-aigua*. It is a soup of cabbage, peas, possibly carrots and meat, with plenty of stock that you mop up with very thin slices of dry bread. As for the fine sauces

that are supposed to have been created on the island, they have French palates to thank for these: the island cuisine remains straightforward, very local and nothing fancy.

You will already be greeted by veritable mountains of *ensaimadas* when you arrive at the airport. These deliciously light spirals of pastry come in various sizes and with various fillings, such as *cabello de ángel* (pumpkin jam), *crema* (confectioner's cream) and *nata* (whipped cream), and are to be found in almost every bakery. The name *ensaimada* comes from *saim* (lard) and means that, for them to be the genuine article, they have to have been deep-fried in lard. *Crespells*, on the other hand, are dry and very crumbly so watch out how you eat them.

The most popular sausage on the island is the *sobrasada*, a sausage for spreading made from pork and the red peppers that

From "salsa de Mahón" to mayonnaise

Whole volumes have been published on the origin of one of the world's most widespread sauces; quite a few of the trails lead to the kitchens of Menorca. And in fact the French Marshal Richelieu, who was certainly not unfavourably disposed to the pleasures of the pillow and the palate, could well have helped mayonnaise to achieve its worldwide popularity. One story goes that there was a young lady of Mahón (a *mahonesa* in Spanish) who stole the Marshal's heart, and let slip to him some of the secrets of Menorcan cuisine. Among the culinary customs of the country that the lady passed on there was a plain, rather rustic potion with which, after a hard day's work, the local peasants fortified themselves before embarking on a hard day's night: olive oil, beaten together with egg, a pinch of salt and crushed garlic. It is quite conceivable that "mayonnaise" resulted from the sauce of the *mahonesa* and from the posh French version (without garlic) of the *all i oli* (garlic and oil) of the Balearics.

"Ensaimadas" and *"tortells"*: at their best fresh from the oven

give it its characteristic red colour. Also on sale everywhere you get *butifarrones* (blood sausages) and *carn i xulla* (a very coarse salami with pepper), as well as plenty of *queso menorquín*, the local cheese.

As surely as gin came to Menorca with the British, just as surely the Menorcans acquired a taste for it, only here everyone knows it as *ginet*. In fact the distillery down by the harbour in Mahón still makes it today and has even carried on using the old recipes. One popular island cocktail goes under the name of *pellofa*, which is *ginet* toned down with a good squirt of soda and the zest of a lemon. Another favourite, particularly on high days and holidays, is a *pomada* – gin with a lemonade mixer.

Herbes (*hierbas* in Spanish), the aromatic herb liqueur, originally hails from neighbouring Ibiza, but you can get a very good version of it on Menorca as well. As a rule this contains up to 40 different herbs and has a typical flavour of aniseed and wild thyme. It comes in three grades: *dulce* (sweet), *semi* (medium dry), and *seco* (dry). *Palo*, a syrupy sweet liqueur made from carob seeds, is also typical of the island. It owes its slightly bitter taste and fever-abating properties to the addition of Cinchona bark which contains quinine. The sugar is melted down in special copper vessels and then displaced with alcohol. The secret of when the sugar reaches boiling point is known only to the experts, but the decisive factor seems to be exactly at what moment the *palo* is removed from the heat.

Costume jewellery and much more

Family businesses and small workshops develop classical elegance with a modern touch

Despite being given up for lost, handicrafts have recently made quite a comeback in the Balearics, and what is happening on Menorca is a good example. New creative minds are taking a fresh look at classic forms, traditional features, and old production processes. The result is there to see: shoes made from good quality leather, in elegant designs, or, less classic, hand-tailored *avarques* (sandals), leather bags, coats, jackets and trousers to suit every taste and every purse. There is also a choice of ceramics, with lovely old hand-painted motifs, and a growing supply of expertly crafted joinery and traditional musical instruments. The latter particularly strike a chord in Ciutadella where they are the speciality of the workshops operated by *Miguel Florit (C/. Sant Nicolau, 111)* and *Joan Benejam (C/. Maó, 82)*. It is some years ago now that an advertising agency and a number of young artists came up with the initiative of printing highly

Leather shoes are top favourites as Menorcan souvenirs

imaginative T-shirts. Nowadays there are shops specializing in this kind of thing in Ciutadella, Mahón, and, most recently, also Palma de Mallorca. Menorca motifs are "in". And, what is more, the island's ceramics and leather are also being exported to its larger neighbouring island: in 1994 a shop selling Menorcan handicrafts actually opened up on Palma's exclusive Jaume III shopping street.

In anywhere of any size in Menorca you will find *bisutéria,* i.e. places selling costume jewellery. This is usually made by families or in small firms, and is part of a tradition dating back to the 17th century when they were turning out fashion accessories – ranging from earrings to belt buckles – on the island. The main centres are Alaior (copper and brass jewellery in the *Bisutería Alben, C/. Maó,* and at *Pons Timoner, C/. Miguel de Cervantes, 36,* mainly for export), Puig de Olives (silversmith *Taller Pere Massa*), Ciutadella (retail factory outlets at *López Freijomil, Plaça Palmers,* or *Fils de Bernardo Marques, C/. Antoni Claret, 23*) and Mahón (factory showroom

"Ginet" is a lasting legacy of the British on Menorca

and sales at *Fábrica Chapado Oro Vid, Polígono Industrial).* Menorca even stages its own modest annual costume-jewellery fair in the autumn (September), while in spring (May) there is SEBIME, the costume-jewellery week which includes retail sales and is held in the Mahón exhibition centre.

The official *opening hours* for shops and department stores are *9.30 am–1.30 pm and 5–8 pm.*

Antiques

For antiques (*antigüedades*) that are quite expensive but mostly of an excellent quality: *Mir (C/. Rosari, 9, Mahón), Toni Ramos (C/. J.M. Quadrado, 41, in the mezzanine, Mahón)* and *Saura (C/. Santíssim, 2, Ciutadella).*

Gin, palo, herbes

One typical Menorcan product that should appeal to souvenir

hunters with alcoholic predelictions is the local gin. This arrived here centuries ago with the British Navy and has been appropriated by the islanders in the guise of *ginet.* Another Menorca speciality with a real kick to it is *palo,* a sweet liqueur made from sugar syrup. *Hierbas* or *herbes,* the liqueur containing up to 40 island herbs, actually stems from Ibiza, but for decades no bar on Menorca would be complete without it. Note that it comes in three degrees of sweetness if you want it as a souvenir: *dulce* (sweet), *semi* (medium dry), and *seco* (dry).

Hand-made firearms

The firm of Denix exports its rifles and handguns to some 40 countries. These are purely collectors' items modelled on pieces that are on show in museums or in the cream of private collections. It is often very hard to tell the replica from the original, though, as the minute engraving is copied right down to the very last detail. Denix products are on sale in souvenir shops, and prices per model range between Ptas 4000 and 15,000; *Denix S.A., Ciutadella, Polígono Industrial, J, Tel. 971 38 15 61*.

Camomile

Menorca's medicinal camomile (*camomilla* in Catalan) used to be professionally harvested and marketed, particularly around Ciutadella. Nowadays unfortunately only a little of it gets picked, but you can still buy genuine Menorca camomile – and other herbs – from *Es Fonoll* in *Mahón (C/. Esglèsia, 16)*.

Capers

The caper bushes have long since conquered the fortifications of Ciutadella and have also taken over nearly everywhere else on Menorca – in old walls, on rugged tablelands, and down steep mountainsides. Their large pale yellow flowers are particularly striking in spring, and then when you look more closely you can spot the flower buds, the actual capers. Once they have been pickled in salt and vinegar in the way that the Menorcans do it every spring, they count as one of the island's choicest delicacies. You are free to pick as many as you want on any open wasteland and that includes on Punta Nati by the lighthouse.

Cheese

The *fromatge de Menorca*, as it has officially been called since 1995, which is also known as *Queso de Mahón*, the brand name that it is sold under, has hardly any smell, has a more or less hard rind, and, thanks to its shape, is easy to carry and to store. Menorca cheese make an ideal holiday souvenir which you can get in virtually every grocery store or direct from the producer. About 30 per cent is home-made. You can tell these cheeses from their industrial counterparts by the marks – particularly on the rounded corners – left by the cotton cloths used in the cheese-making process, and by the stamp denoting *denominación de origen* (of designated origin).

Ceramics

Menorca offers a wide choice of ceramics. The individual pieces or complete sets of tableware are nearly always painted by hand. This is mostly in bright, colourful rustic designs, but you will also find some less ornate English patterns too. Production of the earthenware follows rigid traditional rules; more recently, however, a few young potters have turned to making more creative pieces. Typical earthenware in Menorca and the other islands of the Balearics includes *ollas* and *greixoneras*, cooking pots and dishes, and *bòtils*, stoneware bottles in various shapes and sizes.

Leather

Shoes and leather goods produced on the island are for sale in *Mahón*, for example, at *Milady (Moll de Llevant, 305,* and *C/. Nou, 37)* and at *Pons (C/. Infanta, 7; shoes)*, in *Alaoir* at *Gomila (C/. Miguel de Cervantes, 46; shoes)*, in *Ciutadella* in *Leo (in the Polígono Industrial; leather factory)* and at *looky (Ses Voltes, 14)*, and in *Ferreríes* at *Rubrica (in the Polígono Industrial)*.

Fun on the Feast of St John

Horses and horsemen feature in Menorca's colourful fiestas

The Menorcans are actually supposed to be rather cool characters so far as their Mediterranean temperament is concerned, but in June at least this hots up with a good shot in the arm from the feast of Saint John. The fiesta of "Sant Joan" in Ciutadella is one of the highlights in the entire Spanish calendar of holidays and festivals, and people travel to it from Mahón, from Mallorca, and even from the mainland. The guilds are supposed to have processed through the streets for this event way back in the Middle Ages. Initially they were accompanied by the Knights of Malta in full armour, then in later generations their place was taken by mounted members of the town gentry. Little more is known about the fiesta's origins in any detail since the town archive fell victim to the Turks in 1558. The protocol governing the current order of events dates back to 1611. And now, as then, the sweating horses still tear through the heaving throng, there is fun, frolic and flirting –

People flock to see the horses and riders when Ciutadella celebrates the feast of St John

and drinking too, often, for some, more than is good for them. The accident statistics – published "the morning after" in the daily news every year – are a salutory indication that having such a good time also comes at a price. Horses also take part in many of the other *festes* and *jaleos* on Menorca. There were 147 horses in Ciutadella for the feast of St John in 1996, plus 35,000 visitors (17,000 of them from Mallorca or the mainland), as well as the town's own population of 21,000.

PUBLIC HOLIDAYS

1 Jan *Año Nuevo*, New Year
6 Jan *Los Reyes Magos*, Epiphany
March/April *Jueves Santo*, Maundy Thursday, *Viernes Santo*, Good Friday
1 May *Día del Trabajo*, Labour Day
May/June *Corpus Christi*, Corpus Christi
25 July *Sant Jaume*, Feast of St James
15 Aug *Asunción de María*, Assumption
12 Oct *Día de la Hispanidad*, Discovery of America Day
1 Nov *Todos los Santos*, All Saints

MARCO POLO SELECTION: EVENTS

1 **Festes de Sant Joan in Ciutadella**
Visitors flock from throughout the island to the feast of St John with its equestrian events (page 30)

2 **Festes de la Verge de Gràcia in Mahón**
The thanksgiving celebrations for the island's patron culminate in a grand firework display (page 31)

6 Dec *Día de la Constitución*, Constitution Day
8 Dec *Concepció Imaculada*, Immaculate Conception
25 Dec *Navidad*, Christmas Day
26 Dec *Sant Esteve*, Feast of Stephen

FESTIVALS & LOCAL EVENTS

January
17, Ciutadella: *Festa de Sant Antoni*, Feast of St Anthony; *Processió d'es tres Tocs*, procession to commemorate the recapture of Menorca from the Moors by King Alfonso III of Aragón in 1287

February
Carnaval; a modest version of Carnival takes place in Ciutadella and Mahón

March
19, Ferreríes: *Día de Sant Josep*, feast of St Joseph; auction of typically decorated bread

March/April
Setmana Santa, Holy Week; the leading procession is the *Processió del Sant Enterrament* on Good Friday in Mahón; on Easter Monday folk groups sing on the streets and in churches throughout the island

May
8, Es Mercadal: *Festa de la Verge del Toro*; the feast of the Virgin of Monte Toro includes a solemn mass followed by a procession in honour of the town's patron saint

May/June
Pentecostés, Whitsun: usually outings to the country, often combined with a grand picnic for all the family

June
★ Sunday before *Sant Joan*, St John, Ciutadella: start of the St John fiesta with the *Día d'es Be*; highpoint of the *Festes de Sant Joan* on the 23rd and 24th.
29, Port de Maó: *Festa de Sant Pere*, fiesta in honour of St Peter, patron saint of fishermen; fishing boats assemble in the harbour

July
9, Ciutadella: festival commemorating the attack by the Turks in 1558; readings from the *Llibre Vermell*
15/16, Mahón, Ciutadella and Fornells: processions with ships and fishing boats in honour of Our Lady of Mount Carmel
24/25, Es Castell: *Festa de Sant Jaume*, fiesta in honour of St James the Elder
3rd Sunday, Es Mercadal: *Festa de Sant Martí*, fiesta in honour of

St Martin; processions and riding contest; by ancient custom typical local specialities are handed out to everyone on St Martin's Day

Last weekend, Fornells: town fiesta

August

1st weekend, Es Migjorn Gran: *Festa de Sant Cristòfal*, fiesta in honour of St Christopher; Llucmaçanes: *Festa de Sant Gaietà*, fiesta in honour of St Gaetano

2nd weekend, Alaior: *Festa de Sant Llorenç*, fiesta in honour of St Laurence; with luck you could be one of those who get sprinkled with holy rose-water

3rd weekend, Sant Climent: *Festes de Sant Climent*, fiesta in honour of St Clement, the town's patron saint

23–25, Ferreríes and Ciutadella: *Festes de Sant Bartomeu*, fiestas in honour of St Bartholomew; the fiesta in Ferreríes is more authentic

4th weekend, Sant Lluís: *Festes de Sant Lluís*, fiesta in honour of St Louis, the town's patron saint, with large craft fair

September

★ 7/8, Mahón: *Festes de la Verge de Gràcia*; the grand celebrations in honour of *La Mare de Deu de Gràcia*, the Madonna of Monte Toro, include processions and equestrian events; in 1994 over 100 horses took part; the finale on the 9th, the *Castell des fog*, is probably the island's largest firework display

November

All Saints Day (*Tòts dels Sants*) is celebrated everywhere by visiting the cemetery; to keep their strength up people eat *bunyols* (deep-fried doughnuts) and *panellets* (pastries with honey and almonds)

The chapel of the Verge de Gràcia on top of Monte Toro

Merry Minorca

Mahón (Maó) is the island capital and the focus of business and local government – thanks to the British

There has been a smouldering feud for centuries between Ciutadella in the west of Menorca and Mahón in the east. Long after the end of the Middle Ages Ciutadella continued to be the island's most important port and hence its leading town. The change came with the arrival of the British who occupied the island and called it Minorca, as many still do today. Resistance to the British occupation grew with each new Governor, especially in

the ranks of the noble families, most of whom had lived in Ciutadella since way back. The clergy, who were mightily put out in any case by the sudden presence of the competing Anglican creed, were angry with Governor Kane for meddling in the affairs of the Inquisition, the strong right arm of their Church. In fact, the English dignitary's official receptions in Ciutadella for the representatives of the Church and the Nobility must have proceeded very icily indeed. In Mahón it was quite different.

View of Mahón and its harbour

Hotel and restaurant prices

Hotels
Category 1: over Ptas 7000
Category 2: Ptas 3000 to 7000
Category 3: up to Ptas 3000
The prices are per person for one night; breakfast is usually included.

Restaurants
Category 1: over Ptas 2200
Category 2: Ptas 1500 to 2200
Category 3: up to Ptas 1500
The prices are for a main course plus a drink, or for a whole menu.

Abbreviations

	Menorcan	**Spanish**	**English**
Avda.	Avinguda	Avenida	Avenue
C/.	Carrer	Calle	Street
Ctra.	Carretera (Camí)	Carretera	Road
Ptas.	Pesetes	Pesetas	Pesetas

Here the English were received almost as liberators, who also opened up the prospect of new ideas and additional business opportunities. So Richard Kane probably hesitated only briefly before, without more ado, he made the more receptive Mahón capital of the island. Since that time it has been the hub of Menorca's trade, the seat of justice and local government, and the island's most important port.

ES CASTELL

(105/E4) The little township at the entrance to the long fjord-like estuary leading up to Mahón demonstrates, with its tidy town plan and garrison buildings surrounding the central main square, how much of an impact English colonial rule had on the architecture here. Built as Georgetown by the British to serve as their army base on the island, it was later renamed Villacarlos and then finally Es Castell and is now a confident and flourishing community (pop. 4630). The little harbour, *Cales Fonts*, is a lively place, buzzing with bars, boutiques and tiny restaurants, and, after dark, takes on a large share of Mahón's nightlife.

RESTAURANTS

Rocamar
One of Menorca's top restaurants so far as carefully prepared fish and seafood dishes are concerned, with the emphasis on *langosta*. The service is obliging, the prices are high. *Open daily except Sun evening, C/. Fonduco, 32, Tel. 971 36 56 01, category 2*

Trébol
The small waterfront restaurant is also highly thought of by the Menorcans, especially for its fresh fish. *Cales Fonts, 43, Tel. 971 36 70 97, category 2*

SHOPPING

The market is Mon and Wed 9 am–1 pm. Handicrafts mostly feature glass: *Piedad Valderrey Dueñas, C/. Sant Jaume, 2a, Tel. 971 35 19 60*

HOTELS

El Almirante

This 18th-century house, at one time the home of Nelson's friend, Admiral Collingwood, is now a hotel open to everyone. Close to the sea, tennis court and swimming pool. *38 rooms, Ctra. Port de Maó – Es Castell, Tel. 971 36 27 00, Fax 971 36 27 04, category 2*

Rocamar

Right on the sea, with a view of the port, and less than 3 km from Mahón; for anyone with a hire car this hotel, with its family-friendly atmosphere, is well worth considering as an alternative to staying somewhere in Mahón. *22 rooms, C/. Fonduco, 32, Tel. 971 36 56 01, Fax 971 36 52 99, category 2*

SPORT

Sailing classes in the *Club Náutico Es Castell* (25 moorings, water, power, no fuel pumps), *Miranda de Cales Fonts, Tel. 971 36 58 84*

ENTERTAINMENT

In the district around Cales Fonts, the pace is humdrum rather than high-life; small shops open until late at night, little bars, relaxed cafés, and restaurants with an international air make for a pleasant atmosphere for a quiet evening out among people. Places mentioned include the *Mermelada* (dance bar with mixed audience, *Urbanización Sol del Este*) and the *Flintstones* (smart disco with good music, not too noisy, and international crowd, central location, *C/. Sant Jordi, 10*).

INFORMATION

Town hall, Tel. 971 36 51 93

SURROUNDING AREA

Trips round the harbour on *El Pirata*, a small diesel-engined *llaut*, the traditional fishing boat of the Balearics, twice a day – morning and afternoon – in summer, from *Cales Fonts.*

Castell de Sant Felip   (105/E4)

The road to the cemetery (*Camí del Cementeri*) also leads to the ruins of the fortress that once dominated the entrance to Mahón harbour. King Philip II of Spain felt there was only one way of giving protection against the constant threat of pirates, and that was to build fortifications. The work began in May 1554 but was not finished until 54 years later – and then only provisionally since the British went on to build up the fort to become one of the most secure of its kind in the whole Mediterranean. It was so secure that when Charles III came to the throne he ordered the fortress to be blown up. Nowadays you can see the ruins which are slowly but surely being reclaimed by nature, underground galleries and connecting passageways, as well as a Military Museum housed in a former gunpowder store (*Museo Militar, open Sat/Sun 11 am–1 pm*).

The south bank of nearby *Cala Sant Esteve* holds another fortress. This is where the British built *Fort Marlborough* (1710–1716), and it too had a whole labyrinth of underground passages. The entire area is now a protected military zone with limited access.

Illa del Llatzeret   (105/E–F4)

The southern tip of the island at the entrance to the harbour is covered by an enormous hospital which between 1807 and 1917 served as the quarantine station for the port. Strongly guarded and sheltered by massive walls the hospital must have lived through countless tragedies. As evidence that the hospital chaplains were also by no means immune to fatal epidemics there is the invention of the "host machine" whereby Father Francisco Preto was able to administer holy communion without coming into bodily contact.

In addition to the lazaret, which is used by the Spanish Ministry of Health for conferences and as a health spa for civil servants, there is also a small *museum*. Boats leave three times a week in summer *(Thu, Fri, Sat)* from *Cales Fonts*.

MAHÓN (MAÓ)

☛ **City Map inside back cover**

(105/D–E4) English features from way back are not only built into the façades of many of Mahón's houses but they are also there to be seen in the faces of its people. At every turn in the lively island capital (pop. 22,100) you can see and feel that the British were masters of Menorca for almost a hundred years, and have left behind not just signs of their lifestyle and way of thinking, but many physical features as well. The telltale signs include square jaws, red hair and wiry frames, and often it is only the clothing or the language that tells you whether someone is an islander or a Brit on holiday.

The Plaça de S'Esplanada is also English in origin. All the main roads end here, and this is the best place to leave your car if you have one, since – apart from the underground car park beneath the square and some spaces in the surrounding streets – there is very little parking in the town centre. On the square itself, which at one time did duty as the parade ground for the occupying British, children play between the hibiscus bushes in the gardens and tourists rest on the benches after the tiring business of sightseeing. If you need any help, friendly advice will be forthcoming in the tourist information centre on the northern side of the square.

TOUR

The *Carrer de ses Moreres* runs east from the *Plaça de S'Esplanada* into the old part of the town. When it comes to window-shopping, you will find boutiques, souvenir shops, snackbars, and a bronze bust. This depicts an illustrious citizen of Mahón, one Dr. Mateu Orfila; he is said to have been the founder of toxicology – the study of poisons – and, at the Institut Pasteur in Paris, was hailed as one of the leading scientists of his time.

At the end of the avenue the *Carrer Bastió* forks left and the *Costa d'en Deiá* heads off to the right towards the *Plaça Reial* with the *Teatro Principal*, the municipal theatre. Looking straight ahead you can see the city gate through which Redbeard the Pirate stormed into Mahón, bloodily subjugated the town, plundered it, and then carried off over 1000 of its citizens. One dramatic footnote to history: a few traders are supposed to have opened the gates for the pirates to save their own skins. But times passes and people forget and now the city gate and the city walls have also had to give way to modern town planning. The *Carrer Hannover* or, as the Menorcans prefer to call it, the *Costa de Sa Plaça* is another shopping street, where you can buy books, fashions and souvenirs, hamburgers and shoes. Now and again a little bar is squeezed between the shopfronts, and the *Plaça Colón*, with its palms and cobblestones,

also makes a nice change. Here and in the *Carrer Nou*, in the main arteries of the pedestrian precinct, is where people meet at fiesta time, or simply get together over a cup of coffee. While on the subject of coffee, when it comes to breakfast and to *merienda*, that little interval between meals around 10–11 am or 5–5 pm, you will be well looked after in the local bars and cafés. Then, depending on what you fancy, you can enjoy watching the people hurrying by as you indulge yourself with an *ensaimada* and a *café con leche*, or a *tapas variadas* and a cold beer.

The centre of Mahón is given over to pedestrians

Popular "classics" that have been around for years include the *American Bar* (mixed public, *Plaça Reial*), *Café Europa* (try the *tapas*); *Rovellada de Dalt, 68)* and the ⚲ *Granja La Menorquina* (almost always full; *Carrer Rosario, 7).* If you are absolutely determined to stay on the *tapas* trail try your luck in the ♘ *La Morada* bar *(Plaça Bastió, 12)*, where the little titbits are washed down with a *penalty* (a glass of beer).

Via *Plaça Reial* and *S'Arravaleta* – where Mahón's pensioners while away their mornings philosophising on the street benches and youngsters spend the afternoons making their first tentative approaches to the opposite sex – you get to *Plaça del Carme*. If possible be here before midday and allow some time to spare, since here in the old cloisters, the *Claustre del Carme*, is where Mahón holds its market – and the wrought-iron gates clang shut promptly at one o'clock. That is all for the day, except that the faint odour of fish from the nearby ♘ fishmarket *(Mercat des Peix)* still testifies to happenings elsewhere in the square. The market and its hall are a unique affair: the vast arcades of the once holy cloisters, raucous chubby-cheeked market women, fruit, vegetables – yet the venerable colonnades (first built in 1726 and still not quite finished) take all this in their stride; in the course of their history they must already have had to contend with prisoners, judges and yelling schoolchildren. For anyone who wants to savour its small-scale spectacle the thing to do is to drink a *carajillo* (small coffee with a shot of spirits) at *El Trueno*, the

market bar, give a generous tip, and then listen to the ringing of the bells.

On the right of the *Plaça d'Espanya*, with its green gardens and trees, the *Costa de Ses Voltes* snakes down to the harbour; to the left, via the *Carrer Santo Cristo*, you can get back to the shopping street, *Carrer Nou*, and straight ahead to the *Plaça de la Conquesta*, the oldest part of the town. This is where the *Casa de Cultura (House of Culture)* is located, along with a well-stocked public library and the town archive, while a little further on there is the stately if ornate *Ajuntament (Town Hall)*, begun in 1789. You get a good panoramic view of the harbour at the end of the little alleyway, the ◁▷ *Pont d'es Castell.*

The fact that Menorca's earliest inhabitants thought that this more elevated site on the north bank would probably be a good place to settle is borne out, as a testament in stone, by the megalithic finds on the *Plaça de la Conquesta*, and the *talaiot* and *taula* at Trepucó, barely 2 km away. Written testament was later left by the Romans, who also used the safe shelter of the natural harbour. But when it came to growth beyond the city walls, political and legal responsibility, and shopping of a high standard, these things had perforce to await the arrival of the English.

Mahón must have experienced an enormous boom in the 18th century. Old buildings were torn down or converted, and a new standard measurement was introduced as the basis for property tax: this also served as an indication of social class. In the centre of town there are still noticeably three standard widths in terms of the measurement of building façades. Houses that are one *trast* (5 m) wide are on the more modest side and mostly serve as people's homes, bakehouses or little shops. The *trast i mig* (1.5 *trast* = 8 m) typically housed the well-established middle class: prosperous merchants and the better-off civil servants could afford such luxury. The *dos trast* limit (2 *trast* = 10 m and above) was seldom exceeded; this is where the ruling classes flexed their (monetary) muscle. Public buildings and some blocks of flats for well-to-do local families also top the limit.

The British have also left their mark on the "look" of the buildings: many have retained their original "bull's-eye" panes and elegant sash windows, and, as totally convincing proof of the differences in the detail, whereas door knockers in Ciutadella have a fairy-tale quality – there hands, lion's heads, goose-necks, etc. greet you on the doorstep – in Mahón you gain entry by using rather prosaic geometrically-shaped knockers.

Both of Mahón's large churches also stem from the town's heyday. ★ *Santa María*, between *Plaça de la Conquesta* and *Plaça de la Constitució*, was built in and after1748 on the ruins of an older church. At first sight rather simple and unassuming, Santa María's most striking feature actually appeals to the ear rather than the eye. Its spacious Gothic interior houses a real masterpiece of the 19th-century organ-builder's art. Commissioned in 1809 from the Swiss firm of master-craftsmen, Kyburz &

A Swiss masterpiece: Santa María's church organ

Otter, it arrived on the island a year later. With its 3006 pipes and four keyboards it soon became famous throughout Spain, especially for its imitation of the human voice. Organ concerts are staged at irregular intervals (ask in the tourist office). If you do get a chance to hear an experienced organist on one of Europe's most remarkable organs, it really is an opportunity not to be missed. If you just want to take a look at it, the church is open on weekdays *9 am–1 pm and 5–8 pm*.

The building of *Sant Francesc*, Mahón's cathedral, took nearly a century (1719–1792), and this is reflected to some extent in its mixture of architectural styles. Next door is the former Franciscan monastery of *Sant Francesc*, founded in 1439 and now the *Museu de Menorca*. The way there is lined with elegant houses.

You finally get back to the starting point via the gently

ascending *Carrer Sant Roc* which leads to the *Plaça Bastió*. The gate was part of the ancient city walls and the starting point for the long journey to Ciutadella and the western end of the island. Nowadays the left-hand tower houses a consumer protection agency, while the square itself is full of bars and cafeterias.

PORT

"Junio, julio, agosto y Mahón / los mejores puertos del Mediterráneo son" (June, July, August and Mahón – the best ports on the Mediterranean) was how someone who ought to know put it deftly in rhyme. Andrea Doria, Admiral to the King of Spain, had nothing but praise for the attributes of this, his favourite port, which he thought was the safest place to be outside the summer sailing season: sufficient draught, excellent shelter from wind and weather for a whole fleet, and good medical care were among the nautical strengths he cited for the 6 km-long and up to 800 m-wide deep-water harbour. If necessary the whole harbour basin could be blocked off by a fortress (Sant Felip), like putting a cork in a bottle of rum: an ideal military port and the only one of its great size in the Mediterranean.

It is only in more recent times that modern Mahonese landlubbers have started putting the port to what tend to be more civilian uses. Nowadays Baixamar – "down to the sea" – is where you go on pleasure bound. And the waterfront obliges: not just with places to dine, where the standard of gastronomy is getting better all the time, with, of course, fish and seafood in the lead, but also by offerering all kinds of water-based sports activities and a great variety of other things to do by way of entertainment. By day these range from souvenir shops, an aquarium, boat trips and visits to the famous Xoriguer distillery (where they have been producing gin since the 18th century), and then, by night, you can party till the wee small hours in countless discos, bars and pubs, many of them in converted warehouses in the mercantile part of the port.

Baixamar, however, is not just the gentrified quarter around the two prominent harbour moles, the Moll de Ponent in the west which then to the east becomes the Moll de Llevant, and finally the Cala Figuera: it also covers the coastal strip on the opposite, northern, side. This is the domain of the big industrial works, warehouses and office buildings, and where the ferries berth and take on their passengers; one of its least attractive features is Menorca's solitary power station; this only supplies part of the island, and the rest of the energy is piped in from Mallorca via underwater cable.

Mahón is apparently not looking to this less lovely side of the harbour for its future. Or so it would seem, since what other explanation could there be for the project to extend the Port de Maó around such a grandiose leisure marina, which would catapult the town at a stroke into first place in the island's comparative size stakes.

MUSEUMS

Aquari

To date Menorca has been denied a marine biology research station; this was set up around a century ago on the neighbouring island of Mallorca. But it does have its aquarium instead. This mainly features the life-forms of the Mediterranean and is well worth a visit for anyone with even a passing interest in the underwater world around the island. *By the passenger boat station, in the harbour, open Mon–Fri 9.30 am–1 pm and 4–7 pm, Sat until 2 pm, Sun 11 am–1 pm, admission Ptas 300*

Ateneu Científic   (U/E5)

Library and small exhibition of ceramics, ancient maps and fossils. *Sa Rovellada de Dalt, 25, near Plaça de S'Esplanada, open Mon–Sat 10 am–2 pm and 3.30–10 pm*

Colecció Hernández Mora   (U/E4)

Visit this collection if you want to know more about the more recent history of Menorca in general and Mahón in particular. Ancient maps, books, documents, bronze busts and some furniture breathe life back into the long-forgotten days of yore. *In the main hall of the Claustre del Carme, Plaça del Carme, open Mon–Sat 11 am–1 pm*

Museu de Menorca   (U/E4–5)

The building work took twenty years but Menorca's own museum, having been extensively upgraded, finally re-opened, under the auspices of the Balearic Government, at the end of 1995. The former Franciscan monastery of *Sant Francesc*

houses interesting displays of ethnological, historical, and archaeological finds. Thus Menorca's richest fund of traditions, customs, and folk art is finally accessible to the public again. *Plaça des Monestir, open Tue–Fri 10 am–1 pm and 6–9 pm, Sat/Sun mornings only*

RESTAURANTS

Apart from the *Club Marítim*, which is constantly being recommended (**U/F1;** fish, terrace with superb view of the harbour; *Moll de Llevant, table reservation, Tel. 971 36 42 26, category 1–2*), there are plenty of good restaurants in and around Mahón. If all you feel like is a snack, probably the best *ensaimadas* in town, plus other excellent local pastries, are to be had in the *Sucrería Ca'n Vallés* (**U/E4**; *C/. Hannover, 19*).

Gregal   (U/E2)

Simple, clean, well-run, with a Greek owner and a Greek slant to the menu; the speciality is fish. *Moll de Llevant, 306, Tel. 971 36 66 06, category 1*

Jardín Marivent   (U/E2)

Waterfront restaurant with pleasant atmosphere, specializes in fish. *Moll de Llevant, 314, Tel. 971 36 90 67, category 1–2*

Pilar   (U/E5)

❂ Menorcan cuisine with the personal touch. Specialities: vol-au-vent with *butifarrón* and tomato purée filling. *C/. Cardona y Orfila, 61, Tel. 971 36 68 17, category 1*

Pizzaría Roma   (U/E2–3)

✝ Probably Mahón's most popular pizzeria; normal prices. *Moll de Llevant, 295, category 3*

La Tropical (U/F5)

Menorcan cuisine but with some obvious concessions to "European" tastes. *C/. Lluna, 36, Tel. 971 36 05 56, category 2–3*

SHOPPING

The market (mainly handicrafts) is *Tue and Sat 9 am–1 pm* on the *Plaça de S'Esplanada*. Not to be missed: the market hall, *Mercat del Claustre del Carme* (**U/D4**); *daily except Sun 8 am–1 pm).*

S'Alambic (U/D4)

Typical Menorcan souvenirs in a typical Menorcan house: ceramics, leather, liqueurs, wine, gin, cheese, honey and much more. *Moll de Ponent, 36*

Bodega Ferré (U/D-E4)

All kinds of alcohol on sale. *C/.Ponent, 38*

Cascorder (U/D5)

Handicrafts, ceramics, wickerwork. *Moll de Ponent, 61*

Cerámiques Lora (U/D5)

All kinds of ceramics, *Moll de Ponent, 33–36*

Destilería Gin Xoriguer (U/D4)

Here you can sample Menorcan gin before you buy. They also have a large selection of liqueurs. *Andén del Ponent, 93*

José María Irla Pi (O)

Handicrafts, calligraphy artworks and engravings. *Urbanización Horizonte, Vía Estrellas, 4*

José Francisco Lora Buzón (U/D4)

Here the whole family is involved in the ceramics business, making traditional wares hand-painted with simple rustic motifs; relatively low prices. Shopping can be combined with a look round the studios. *Andén del Ponent, 36*

Miguel Martínez (O)

Children's toys, especially wooden ones. *C/. Roig, 19*

Antonio Mullarach Farras (O)

Furnishings, fine fabrics, some of them produced in-house. *C/. Andrea Doria, 24*

The Army publishes good maps

Good maps of Menorca that are really up to date are hard to find. Even the relatively expensive tourist maps of the island often miss out streets in new developments and some of the lovely footpaths. The free maps handed out by the tourist office necessarily only give a general picture. So a word to the wise: throughout Spain the Army also places the findings of its "Geographical Service" (*Servicio Geográfico del Ejército*)at the disposal of civilians. Their maps are quite cheap too, and available to anyone who can produce their passport. There are single maps on the scale of 1:100,000 and a series of maps on the scale of 1:50,000 and 1:25,000. The cartographic department is in *Mahón, Costa de Deiá, 4.*

Musupta Piel (O)
Original designer models in leather and suede. C/.Calvo Sotelo, 26

Lluís Puig Olives (U/D5)
The work of silversmiths. C/. Isabel II, 32

El Turronero (U/E4)
This is the best place to come if you are looking for edible souvenirs of Menorca. Besides sweetmeats (turrones) and their own excellent make of ice-cream, the selection on offer also includes gin, cheese and the island's sausages. C/. Nou, 24

Francisco Vanrell Olives (O)
Enamels, which can also be made to order. C/. Bajoli, 56, Polígono Industrial, Tel. 971 36 27 30

HOTELS

Capri (U/E6)
Three-star hotel right in the centre of town, very comfortable, almost de luxe; rooms with television and minibar. Mainly used by business travellers. 87 rooms, C/. Sant Esteve, 8, Tel. 971 36 14 00, Fax 971 35 08 53, category 1

Residencia Jume (U/E4)
🏃 ☺ This is a cheap place to stay even if that means only limited mod cons. It has had a reputation for years as good reliable accommodation and is particularly popular with youngsters who are over here from the Spanish mainland. 42 rooms, C/. Concepció, 4–6, Tel. 971 36 32 66, Fax 971 35 48 34, category 3

Port Mahón (O)
〽 A four-star establishment and probably Mahón's best-known and most highly rated hotel. It has a superb view over the marina and out to sea. Completely renovated and extremely well appointed, it is cetainly not cheap. Air conditioning, swimming pool, minibar. 74 rooms, Fort de l'Eau, 13, Tel. 971 36 26 00, Fax 971 35 10 50, category 1

SPORT

Sailing
There are three places in Mahón where you can both learn to sail (sailing certificates) and rent a sailing boat: Menorca Náutica (yachts and motorboats), Moll de Llevant, 163, Tel. 971 35 45 43, Fax 971 35 32 26; Yrisha Charters (rental of dinghies and boardsails), Moll de Ponent, Berth 67, Tel. 908 63 85 57 (mobile); Samba (sailing school, yacht trips, yachting group excursions, training), C/. Bonaire, 19, Tel. 971 35 29 02 and 908 63 09 11 (mobile).

Tennis
Tenis Mahón (public tennis courts, floodlighting), C/. Trepucó, 4, Tel. 971 36 57 03

ENTERTAINMENT

The western part of the harbour around the 🏃 Moll de Ponent offers plenty of opportunities – particularly for the young – to shake a leg. Here there is a whole host of bars, caf,s and remodelled waterfront pubs all geared to adventure after dark. Very much in fashion, especially with the locals: the ☺ Café Mediterráneo, the Drake, the Cadewe, kind of art nouveau, the Baixamar, for the very young the 🏃 Akelarre and the

Ikaro, for the not so young any more, the *Tríptic*.

The eastern part of the harbour quarter around the *Moll de Llevant* is quieter, more established and more international. Here you can drink a final *cortado* on the terrace of the *Club Marítimo*, or go for a long-drink in the *Oh-la-la* or in the *Café Alba*. *Es Fosquet* offers a large selection of *tapas* as well. If you are after more music, you should try the *Chocolate (C/. Alaior, 14)*, a disco bar with atmosphere and plenty of punters until the early hours *(until 4 am in summer)*. For somewhere quieter there is the *Bar Nou*, with billiard table *(C/. Nou, 1, 1st floor)*. Another place for the young: the ☂ *Kyu (Moll de Llevant, 60)*.

Something that takes a bit of getting used to, but which is not without its charm, is the ☯ *Jazzcava*, normally with live music on Thursday and dancing at the weekend *(Plaça Príncipe, 12a)*. The *Café Mirador*, which owes its name (look-out point) to the ⌁ view of the harbour from the terrace, is full of life from morning till late at night; the speciality of the house is *bocatas* (rolls) with all kinds of fillings, and *tapas* *(Plaça d'Espanya, 2)*.

INFORMATION

Oficina de Información turística
Plaça de S'Esplanada, 40, Tel./Fax 971 36 37 90

BUSES

Bus stop for the journey to Ciutadella: on the *Plaça de S'Esplanada*. Buses run there several times a day, but the frequency depends very much on the season. Information via *Tel. 971 38 03 93* (in Spanish) or from the tourist information centre.

There are also regular services from Mahón to Es Castell, to Sant Lluís, to Es Migjorn Gran, Ferreríes and Cala Galdana, to Sant Climent and Cala En Porter, to Alaior and Son Bou, to Fornells and Arenal d'en Castell, to Sant Cristòfal and Sant Tomás.

USEFUL ADDRESSES & TELEPHONE NUMBERS

- Town hall: *Tel. 971 36 98 00*
- Airport information: *Tel. 971 36 01 50*
- Free information about Mahón: *Tel. 900 30 05 84*
- Taxi switchboard: *Tel. 971 36 71 11, 971 36 12 83 and 971 36 28 91*
- Red Cross emergency number: *Tel. 971 36 11 80*
- Police emergency: *971 36 11 00 and 091*
- Head post office: *C/. Bonaire, 15*
- Car rental: *Europcar, Plaça de S'Esplanada, 8, Tel. 971 36 06 20, Fax 971 36 89 65*
- Motorcycles and bicycles: *Motos Menorca, Cuesta de General, 18, Tel. 971 36 73 09* (motorcycles cost around Ptas 2000 a day, insurance and helmet included)

SURROUNDING AREA

Harbour cruises mainly concentrating on Port de Maó: departure in summer daily in the harbour by the *Destilería Gin Xoriguer*, the *Yellow Boats* operated by the *El Menorquí* shipping company are mostly larger than the *El Pirata* boat.

Island cruises with *Líneas de la*

Cruz go to many remote beaches and swimming coves that are often virtually inaccessible by road or on foot. The shipping line also runs some glass-bottomed boats along large sections of the coast. Day cruises start from Mahón in the north-east via *Sa Mesquida* to the *Illa d'en Colom* and to the *Es Grau Nature Reserve*, and, in the south, via *Punta Prima, Cales Coves, Son Bou* and *Cala Galdana* to *Cala En Turqueta*; in summer the boat stops so you can go for a swim. During the summer the boats set out to sea *daily at 10 am*, and get back at around *5 pm*. Departure in Port de Maó opposite the aquarium. Ticket sales: *Aquarium Tel. 971 35 05 37*.

Golden Farm (105/E3)

In the famous 18th-century Georgian style, its architecture is English, its name is English, and the stories about it are English too. One that you are bound to hear is about Lord Nelson and Lady Hamilton. It all sounds very romantic: England's great admiral is supposed to have spent just six days here while bad weather kept his ship in port in Menorca, and during that time Lady Hamilton was evidently in Italy, but who knows – perhaps there was a clandestine rendez-vous … Golden Farm is not open to the public. The best view of it is a glimpse of the façade on the seaward side; a path leads down from the house to the sea.

Illa del Rei (105/E4)

The massive hospital complex that, to this day, covers most of this island was commissioned by Governor Kane. From when it was built in the 18th century the building remained virtually unchanged and continued to serve as a hospital right up to the 1950s. There are plenty of sinister tales about the island which the jolly jack tars were already calling *Bloody Island* over two centuries ago – the spare parts left over after surgery are supposed to have been thrown straight into the sea. In 1986 Mahón Town Council was tendering for the building to become the site of some kind of public institution. There was talk of a genetic research centre, of a museum, Elton John wanted to go and live there, the Balearics Power Company wanted a laboratory, speculators thought it would be a good site for a hotel. Ten years later, in 1996, the building still stood empty. Illa del Rei also has the remains of an early Christian basilica, but its main attraction – a relatively well preserved mosaic – is on display in the Casa de Cultura in Mahón.

Sa Mesquida (105/E3)

The bay and fishing village are mainly the preserve of the Menorcans themselves – this is where the Mahonese swim and sunbathe. Holidaymakers may not be excluded but clearly this is not their territory. The shoreline which stretches for some 700 metres is divided in two by a tongue of land. The larger beach is around 300 metres long but not particularly suitable for children since it shelves steeply. Incidentally Sa Mesquida is where the French and Spanish set out from in 1781 to recapture the island, reason enough for the British to secure the bay with their own fortress in 1798. A restaurant to look out for: *Cap Roig (Tel. 908 63 65 93 (mobile), summer only, category 2)*; comfy terrace with view of the sea. The owner guarantees that any fish is fresh that day.

Es Murtar (105/E3)

Used more for angling than swimming, this cove, enclosed in black slate, is mostly quiet and with few people around; the ground slopes gently away.

Talaiot de Trepucó (105/E4)

About 2 km south of Mahón, this prehistoric settlement is frequently reckoned to be the site with the most spectacular *taula* – this one is over 4.20 m tall – and the largest *talaiot* (40 metres in length) in the Balearics. Six other stone towers that were mentioned in the ancient chronicles have since vanished; they may have provided some of the building materials for the ramps and barricades built for the French Governor in 1781 so that the artillery could train their guns on the fortress of Sant Felip from here.

Talatí de Dalt (113/D4)

This well preserved – and well restored – ancient settlement was inhabited up until the time of the Roman occupation. The standing stones supporting the massive stone that crowns the *taula* are particularly striking. The way there is signed at km 4 on the road from Mahón to the airport.

SANT CLIMENT

(104–105/C-D4) Of late this is becoming a favourite suburb for Mahón's middle class to move into since, though barely 10 kilometres out of town, it already has that "country life" feeling to it. Things to see are the *Basílica des Fornas de Torelló* with a 6th-century mosaic, and the *Talaiot de Torelló* (both on the left of the road from Sant Climent to Mahón, shortly before the exit to the airport/*Aeroport*). Quite close by there is also a manor house which on closer inspection reveals traces of art nouveau; this is known as *Curnia* and is said to have been the project of one of the pupils of Barcelona's leading exponent of art nouveau, Antonio Gaudí. Behind the main building there is another *talaiot* (*Talaiot de Curnia, km 2.8*).

RESTAURANT

Es Molí de Foc
Good international cuisine with French nuances, housed in an old, well-restored mill; pleasant atmosphere. *C/. Sant Llorenç, 65, Tel. 971 15 30 13, category 2*

SHOPPING

Josefina Egea Gómez
Ceramics from their own workshop. *C/. Binixica, 166*

SPORT

Picadero Doble C
Riding club. *Road to Cala En Porter, Tel. 971 36 42 31*

ENTERTAINMENT

Restaurante Casino San Clemente
A pleasant place to dine and a good British ambience; on Tues-

day and Thursday evenings in summer live jazz from 9.30 onwards. *C/. Sant Jaume, 4, Tel. 971 15 34 18, category 1*

INFORMATION

Tourist information centre in Mahón

SURROUNDING AREA

Cala En Porter   (104/B4)

On the left you have an unspoilt natural landscape, seen from the sea, but on the right the slope is taken up with a holiday village. The beach at the end of the bay is around 400 metres wide, with fine sand, and a gentle slope down into the sea, ideal for the whole family – and the word has certainly already got about.

Further inland a good place to stay is the *Hostal Sa Payssa* (very obliging service, good mod cons, reasonable prices, sun terrace, swimming pool, mainly English clientele, dogs allowed); *26 rooms, Via Principal, Tel. 971 37 73 89, no Fax, category 3).* A good place for ceramics and costume jewellery: *Andreu's (C/. Xaloc, Edficici Mediterrani, Local 2).*

A first-rate attraction, especially in the evening, is the ◁▷ *Cova d'en Xoroi* discotheque. In terms of its location, outlook, and atmosphere it is totally unique. Halfway between the sea and the sky, in the rocks that make up the cliff face, you can only get to it via a (properly surfaced) stone path, and once there, you have a breathtaking view of the horizon and the waves. The punters here come from all over the world to avail themselves of the versatile space and other special effects to be found in this vast natural grotto. It comes as no surprise, then, that many famous Menorcan songs and legends feature this place.

Cova d'en Xoroi's cave disco is a major attraction

Cave dwellings down through the ages: the Cales Coves

The best known of these is the following story. After a series of disastrous forays in search of plunder the Moorish pirate Xoroi ("the one-eared") was dumped by his crew on the shores of Menorca. In pursuit of a wild goat he stumbled upon this inaccessible cave by the sea and made it his stronghold. The local peasants were soon spreading the word that a bandit was holed up here somewhere; the odd chicken would go missing, sometimes it would be a whole pig, and at some point a pretty young peasant girl also vanished without trace. The anger of the peasants continued unabated, but they never succeeded in tracking down the thief's hiding place – until years later, one cold winter's night, there was a snowfall on the fields of Menorca and the tracks led straight to the cave. Armed with knives and clubs the peasants stormed the pirate's hideout, whereupon he plunged headlong into the sea. They found the young woman in

the best of health, and with three children who later adopted the surname of Mercadal and settled in the centre of the island. But that is another story … Xoroi the Pirate was never seen again, but centuries later they are still singing his praises and boasting of his bravery, gallantry and love of freedom.

Cales Coves (104/B4)

★ Up until 1995 a clan of backpackers and hippies lived in the caves of Cales Coves as the cave-dwellers had lived three thousand years before them. The hippies who had arrived in ones and twos in the winter had formed a proper colony by the summer. Then in the spring and summer of 1995 the police moved in to repossess the national monument, and the hippies were turned out. The name of the place (i.e. cave coves) is in the plural because the bay is divided into two coves, one of which is fed by freshwater; both are buried deep in the grey rock. The sheltered bay is out of the wind, hence its crystal-clear waters are often as smooth as a sheet of glass, but the access via a gravelled road is very bumpy.

The 150 or so caves have a chequered past. The oldest date from the 11th century B.C. and served as dwellings. Up until the 4th century B.C. they were still digging large caves out of the limestone, often with central pillars and sleeping quarters in the side-caves which usually served as places of habitation as well. Traces of the Romans have also been found. Some of the caves were used for religious purposes, and time and again seafarers – including freebooters – and fishermen used to seek shelter in the bay when it was rough out to sea. Up until very recently the farmers were still using some of the caves as places to keep their livestock.

Es Canutells (104/C5)

For the people who live in Sant Climent this bay serves as the town's "harbour". Its special features include the boatsheds carved out of the rock, and the little sandy beach which you get to via a weathered set of steps. In recent years a settlement above the bay has encroached further and further inland, and only the western edge of the bay has so far remained undeveloped. The road that links Sant Climent to Sant Lluís still boasts a particularly fine example of a Menorcan mixture of architectural styles. The 19th-century manor house, the *Casat de Formet (Forma Vell)*, has a striking red façade and the terraced park in the grounds has an impressive array of water features and fountains.

SANT LLUÍS

(105/D–E5) The little town looks as though it has just been given a new coat of paint and appears fresh as a new pin. White is the dominant colour, the houses all have flat roofs and there is not a soul on the narrow streets, just a couple of children playing under the pinetrees in the park at the entrance to the town, in the shade of the large mill-wheel. The white-washed mill has been restored and contains a modest collection of folk-art (*open daily 9.30 am–1.30 pm, better to telephone beforehand, Tel. 971 15 09 50*). The town has a population of just on 3000, many of them newcomers from Mahón. A growing number of foreigners have also joined the local community here, many with French roots. The place itself is relatively new: Count Lannion, one of the French Governors, founded it during a brief visit to the island in the mid-18th century, when during the French occupation he set about drawing up the ground plan, using pencil and tape measure. The town has a correspondingly geometric ground plan. The church after which the town is named was dedicated to Saint Louis, the French King, but was only completed under British rule after Menorca had been retaken by the English in 1763.

La Caraba

Unusual but tasty dishes using recipes based on the traditional Menorca cuisine but refined by the capable touch of the lady in charge. *Open evenings, C/. S'Vestra, 78, Tel. 971 15 06 82, category 2*

La Rueda

This may only be a bar but the *tapas* here are famous throughout the island. *In the centre of town*

The market is on *Mon and Wed 9 am–1 pm* in the town centre.

Biniali

A dream in white; several white-washed units, interlocking, traditional and yet it has a tiny three-star hotel with swimming pool, lovely sun terrace and family atmosphere. *9 rooms, C/. Ullastrar, 50, Tel. 971 15 17 24, Fax 971 15 03 52, closed November–March, category 1*

There is not much going on in Sant Lluís at night. If you like loud music, go to the ☆ *Tonic* disco pub in a cave just outside the town; mainly local youngsters. The atmosphere is more international at the Pashá disco *(Avda. Generalísimo).*

Town hall, Tel. 971 15 09 50

S'Algar (105/E5)

Holidaying is what S'Algar is all about. Club S'Algar, the water sports centre, offers just about everything you can think of

A 21st-century model fishing village: Binibèquer Vell

50

when it comes to water sports: diving, windsurfing, sailing, water-skiing, waterboarding, etc. Here you can also rent diving gear and sailboats, get scuba-diving equipment and do courses to get certificates for sailing and diving; it is worth asking for group and second-timer rebates (*Club S'Algar Watersports Center, Passeig Marítim, Tel. 971 15 06 01, Fax 971 15 06 04*). If, on the other hand, you prefer peace and quiet, walk round the hill to the north side of the *Cala Rafalet*. The *Picadero Es Boaret* riding stables (*Tel. 971 15 10 49*) can arrange for tours on horseback. Evening entertainment is catered for by *S'Algar Disc*, the hotel disco.

Biniancolla, Binidali, Biniparratx, Binissafúller (104–105/C–E5–6)

The names of the places have their roots in Arabic but their holiday resorts are of very recent origin. Almost every "Cala" has its own little sandy beach. There is a sailing school at Cala Biniancolla (*Menorca Cruising School, Tel. 971 15 17 38*).

Binibèquer Vell (105/D5–6)

★ Menorca's number one tourist attraction on the south-east coast rather resembles an ants' nest. Although the buildings in this "typical fishing village" are more or less brand new, the interlocking alleys, tunnels, twists and turns, nooks and crannies are supposed to be as they would have been dreamt up by earlier fisherfolk. The name of the place, at least, is Arabic in origin. Just before the start of the seaon the whole place is gleaming white, the stone pavements have been cleaned, the souvenir shops and bars are posting their first special offers in the windows – Binibèquer is ready and waiting and all's right with the world. In the peak of the holiday season, though, the narrow alleys can seem very cramped.

Cala d'Alcaufar (105/E5)

This is what all the fishing villages on the island looked like before they were turned into holiday resorts. Cala d'Alcaufar is a simple place, with white boat-sheds right on the sea, and most of the people who live here are Menorcans. A natural break-water at the entrance to the Cala ensures a calm sea. And a hotel to look out for: the *Xuroy*, on the edge of the houses, close to the sea; the simple two-star decor and facilities meet any requirements, and the rates are reasonable too – quiet holidays, far from the madding crowd, are guaranteed (*46 rooms, postal address: Apartado 250, Menorca, Tel./Fax 971 15 18 20, category 3*).

Punta Prima (105/E6)

Sailors may well fear this south cape of the island but for holiday-makers it is always very much a favourite. Punta Prima, one of the pioneers among Menorca's holiday resorts, has a beach of fine white sand that slopes gently into the sea and has plenty of room for sunbathing, so of course it gets lots of visitors. In summer you can get a boat from here to the *Illa de l'Aire*. The 18th-century watch-tower guarding the western edge of the beach is now a youth hostel. It mainly takes young Spaniards in groups of up to 15 (*Information: Oficina de Información juvenil, Mahón, Tel. 971 36 45 34*).

Wilder and greener in the North

Where the wind shapes the face of the earth and the nature of the people

"The *tramuntana* rests not and forgives not", thus runs an old Menorcan saying, and one that probably most tellingly accounts for the bizarre shapes of the coastal rocks, carved from stone by centuries of seaspray and tempest, and the crooked pines that bend before the strong north winds. It also explains why, in the course of the island's history, hundreds of galleons and fishing boats have gone down off the rugged coast between Punta Nati and Cap de Favàritx, and why the people on the north coast of Menorca are quiet and withdrawn by nature. For the *tramuntana* not only shapes the rocks and the trees, it also shapes the people who live here. This driving north wind that gets up from time to time has always been said to have had an effect on the psyche, and recent medical statistics have actually indicated that the wind is linked to a distinct tendency to depression. Be that as it may, some of Menorca's most outstandingly beautiful and tranquil natural beaches are to be found in this part of the island, namely, Cala Tirant, Port d'Addaia, Arenal de Son Saura, Cala Pregonda, Na Macaret …

FORNELLS

(102/B2) ★This is where even the Spanish Royal Family are known to enjoy a *caldereta*, the famous lobster stew which is a particular speciality of Fornells. The setting for it is just right too: a charming sleepy lagoon on the otherwise wild north coast with the old fishing port whose people who have long since enjoyed the reputation of being the best at fishing for spiny lobster in the western Mediterranean. Here "best" refers not only to the size of the catch – the noble crustaceans are shipped from here to Barcelona – but also to the sustainability of their *langosta* fishery since the season is limited to the period from March to October. Fornells (pop. 1500) has no problem combining the elegance of the diners and visitors in their Mercedes and BMW limos with the unpretentiousness of the

The grain harvest is all over for these fields near Es Mercadal

people. But the place does have a third component: in the 1960s the Norwegian artist Arnulf Björndal settled in Fornells and opened the island's first art gallery (since closed) at the entrance to the town. Other painters followed, mainly from elsewhere in Spain and from Scandinavia, with a consequent highly productive "cultural short-circuit".

Fornells itself dates from the 17th century. When Philip IV built a small fort at the entrance to the bay in 1625 a number of fishing families and the inevitable priest soon settled here as well. The fort and the church failed to withstand the test of time – the present church is much more recent (18th century). Every summer from late July to late August it provides the setting for the "Nights of classical music" series of concerts (*Nits de la Música clássica*) which are much enjoyed by locals and visiting residents alike.

RESTAURANTS

Es Cranc
A good place if you like fish.

C/.Escoles, 29, Tel. 971 37 64 42, category 1–2

Es Pla
This is mouthwatering Menorcan haute cuisine, where, as you enjoy the view over the lagoon, you can dine on one of the best *calderetas* on the island. Other dishes cater too much for international tastes though. The number of visiting Menorcan holidaymakers who eat out here in summer is particularly high. The restaurant's lunch menu is relatively cheap. *Pasatje des Pla, Tel. 971 37 66 55, category 1–2*

HOTELS

S'Algaret
Comfortable guest house with air conditioning in the centre of town; all 23 rooms with balcony and telephone. *Plaça de S'Algaret, 7, Tel./Fax 971 37 66 66, category 1–2*

La Palma
Simple "hostal", adjoining a fishing pub; this is just the place if all you need are the bare essentials and are looking for low prices and

a sociable atmosphere. *23 rooms, Plaça de S'Algaret, 3, Tel. 971 37 64 87, Fax 971 37 66 34, category 2*

SPORT

Although it does not have an official yacht station Fornells does have a few moorings; access to water, power points, and showers. Information: *Tel. 971 37 66 04, Urbanización Ses Salines.*

Menorca Country Club
Not right inside Fornells but on the western side of the *Punta Mala*, on the *Cala Tirant*, this apartment hotel with its adjoining sports centre has plenty of sports facilities and these are also open to non-residents. You can hire sailing boats, learn to dive and windsurf, play tennis, go riding and then end up by relaxing in the sauna or in a jaccuzi. *Urbanización Playas de Fornells (Cala Tirant), Tel. 971 37 65 22, Fax 971 37 65 23, open May–Oct*

Servinàutic Menorca
Rental of sailing boats and motor boats, sailing certificates, water skiing. *C/. Major, 27*

Windsurf Fornells
Here you can be taught how to sail and surf by qualified staff; after that, you can also hire surfboards, small dinghies and catamarans. *At the harbour (Port de Fornells), Tel. 971 37 64 58*

INFORMATION

Pedánea de Mercadal de Fornells, C/. Escuelas, 23, Tel. 971 37 66 08, 971 37 64 00

The port of Fornells is where they land prime "langostes"

ENTERTAINMENT

Discerning visitors to Menorca particularly appreciate the evening stroll along the harbour road, especially, for those who can afford it, if their table has already been reserved at one of the renowned restaurants. In August you can also listen to classical music, in the *Church of Sant Antoni (Thursday evenings).*

SURROUNDING AREA

Cala Binimel.là   **(101/F2)**
Not as quiet as the neighbouring cove *Cala Pregonda* (where you have to pay) but quite attractive with its coarser red sand and a small freshwater spring. There is also a bar available.

Cala Tirant   **(102/A–B2)**
To get to Cala Tirant turn left on the outskirts of Fornells and the road takes you to this holiday development on the slopes leading down to the bay; the wide beach is often littered with seaweed brought in on the waves.

The manager of the Menorcan *Fomento de Turismo* tells a story about the first foreigner to settle here. In 1933 the German painter Hans Hartung wanted to build a modest house in the peace and quiet of the lonely cove. The – at that time unheard-of – request aroused so much suspicion among the local people that the Spanish Ministry of Defence even made inquiries to find out whether this determined German gentleman was not just an artist but could perhaps also be a spy. In the end the *Fomento de Turismo* of the day went out on a limb for the

painter. In a letter to the Spanish authorities their feeling was that Herr Hartung ought to be allowed to go ahead, if only "because so far he is the only foreigner who has managed to make a home on Menorcan soil".

Cap de Cavallería   **(102/A1)**
Here on Menorca's "North Cape" is where the brave women of Sóller on Mallorca had their Menorcan counterparts. Between *Cala Tirant* and *Cala Binimel.là* there are the *Cases de la Cavallería* which was where the cavalry was quartered, with an ancient adjoining peel tower. Here in the 16th century two peasant women are said to have managed to keep the marauding Turkish pirates at bay for so long that reinforcements were finally able to arrive

Cova Polida   **(102/C2)**
The cave is only accessible by water; it has a particularly large number of stalactite and stalagmite formations.

ES GRAU

(103/E5) The little fishing port is becoming increasingly popular with the Menorcans, who pack its alleys and waterfront bars, especially at weekends. Its beach, *Platja d'Es Grau*, about a kilometre from the harbour and shaped like an almost perfect semicircle, has fine grey sand, is gently shelving, and is protected from wind and waves by the island of Colom. In summer, though, the bay is used by hordes of sailing and motor boats.

INFORMATION

Tourist information centre in Mahón

Cap de Favàritx appears bleak and forbidding

SURROUNDING AREA

S'Albufera d'Es Grau (103/D-E4-5)

★ The second largest wetland in the Balearics (the largest is Albufera Gran on Mallorca), these marshes were at the heart of the arguments put forward to justify the creation of the *Reserva de la Biosfera*. On 4 May 1995 the island government kept its promise officially to declare the area a nature reserve. In fact the 1790 ha of the Albufera d'Es Grau only narrowly escaped "death by development". In the early 1970s a start was made on *Shangri-La*, a big holiday complex with a golf course on the east bank of the lagoon. After massive protests by the local people the building of the scheme – which had already begun – was brought to a halt, and many of the owners of the holiday homes who had already taken possession were then threatened with expropriation. Nowadays the margins of the shallow waters are home to over 90 species of bird, including osprey, cormorants and herons,

while the large (67 ha) saltwater lagoon itself also holds terrapins, eels, etc. The conservation measures in the Albufera extend to a ban on cars, on camping (that includes caravans too), and on making a fire. There is also a ban on any kind of water or motor sport, but walking within the reserve is allowed. There are facilities for birdwatching and occasional guided tours; these are organized by GOB Menorca (Camí d'es Castell, 138, 1st floor, Mahón), the local equivalent of a wildlife trust. A word of warning, watch out for ticks: there are lots of them about in the hot weather.

Cala de Sa Torreta (103/D-E4)

This cove 3 km north of Es Grau is hard to get to and consequently usually empty of people. It owes its name to an old watch tower; small sandy beach and ◁▷ panoramic view of the *Illa d'en Colom*.

Cap de Favàritx (103/E3)

★ ◁▷ There are magnificent views along the north coast and

Es Mercadal, dominated by the 357 m peak of Monte Toro

far out to sea from this remote and isolated cape, with its lighthouse and bizarre black rock formations.

Illa d'en Colom   (103/E4)

If you want to visit Illa d'en Colom in summer, a little ferry covers the 500 m from Es Grau (leaving from the harbour in front of the *Bar Bernat, from 10 am onwards*). There is really not an awful lot to see on the island though, apart from a basilica that still has to be excavated and some visible ruins which are all that remain of a former lazaret built by the British as a quarantine station.

ES MERCADAL

(102/A3-4) The predilection of the people of Es Mercadal for light bright colours is particularly noticeable when compared with the dark rusty shades in neighbouring Ferreríes. Virtually every house here is painted a gleaming white and the streets are mostly wide and friendly. But what has a particularly pleasant association for the Menorcans is the way Es Mercadal (pop. 3200) caters for families eating out on their high days and holidays: many a wedding, first communion or other family event is celebrated here with a grand meal in one of its large restaurants. The town is also known for its leather goods, especially footwear. This includes the making of *avarques*, which are typical of Menorca and consist of soles made from car tyres with uppers of virtually untreated raw leather.

Molí des Racó

Despite its simple decor and

paper tablecloths this is a good place to eat out for anyone who wants to enjoy authentic Menorcan cuisine; it has the added bonus of being in a 300-year-old mill (with terrace in summer). This has been converted by three brothers, and they also see to it that there is a family atmosphere. *Ctra. General, no number, Tel. 971 37 53 92, category 2*

SHOPPING

The market is held on *Sun 11 am–2 pm (C/. Verge del Monte Toro)*. From mid-June to 10 Sep there are also market stalls *Mon–Sat 6.30–9.30 pm* on the bypass (*Vía Ronda*). Besides the usual farm produce the *mercat* also sells typical Menorcan products and foodstuffs such as cheese, home-made jams and Balearic wines.

Silk paintings and silk-screen prints can be bought from *Miguel González Piñero* who also supplies the various other handicraft markets on the island.

The *avarques* workshop *(taller)* is in the *Carrer Metges Camps, 3, Taller Gabriel Servera*. The confectioner at *Cas Sucrer (Sa Plaça)* is famous throughout the Balearics, and makes an excellent quality of *turrón* (a kind of nougat with marzipan, peanut butter, Turkish honey or chocolate) and *amargos* (almond paste shaped like an almond).

HOTEL

Jeni
This guest house in the centre of Es Mercadal lends itself to a flying visit to the area rather than an extended stay. Simple but clean rooms, with a small pool in the garden, and the cooking is appreciated by residents and non-residents alike. *36 rooms, Miranda del Toro, 81, Tel. 971 37 50 59, Fax 971 37 51 24, category 2*

INFORMATION

Town Hall, Tel. 971 37 50 02

SURROUNDING AREA

Monte Toro   (102/B4)
The highest point on the island, Monte Toro (El Toro) rises up to 357 m above the otherwise only slightly hilly landscape, looking like a hedgehog, with aerials protruding from its back instead of spines. From the top there is a fantastic panoramic view of the whole island, taking in the Tramuntana in the north and the Migjorn in the south, as well as the fishing boats out to sea, for whom it serves as an important landmark while at the same time providing perfect radio and television reception for large parts of Menorca.

A well-contoured road leads up to Monte Toro from the eastern entrance to Es Mercadal, smoothing the way to what was at one time a favourite pilgrim destination. Nowadays those who make the pilgrimage up the "Mount" (*Monte*), as the Menorcans are wont to call it, are mainly here on holiday. The chapel *Mare de Deu del Toro* (begun in 1670) cowers in the shadow of the transmitter masts. This is where the Bishop blesses the whole island every May, since the Madonna here is also the patron saint of Menorca. The hilltop's own catering facilities are supplemented by a souvenir shop selling a good range of typical sausage products, as well as a broad cross-section of Menorcan handicrafts, including ceramics and costume jewellery together with bottles of *ginet (Tienda de Productos artesanales, open June to mid-October daily 10 am–9 pm]*

The "Indian Head", *Sa Roca de S'Indio*, is a natural rock formation but somewhat less spectacular than its fame would lead you to believe. It is visible on the right-hand side just outside the town from the road from that runs from Es Mercadal to Mahón **(102/A4)**.

PORT D'ADDAIA

(102/C3) The bay here is more an inlet, snaking deep inland like a river, and thus providing one of the few harbours on Menorca's north coast. The slopes of the inlet are covered in evergreen bushes, lending a gently drowsy air to the landscape. But do not let this picturesque idyll mislead you; a few kilometres further east (up to Cap de Favàritx) the coast reverts to rugged black rock, carved into bizarre shapes by the sea and the wind down the centuries. A place that is always popular, and that goes for the locals too, is the ✪ *Bar Pins*; the *Addaia* restaurant *(at the entrance to the town, category 2)* offers pizzas and an international menu.

SPORT

Centro de Buceo ULMO

Diving centre with its own courses, dives for the more expert and accommodation;

cylinders refilled, diving gear rental. Open April to November. *Postal address: Apartado de Correos 569, Mahón, Tel. 971 18 89 96, Fax 971 35 90 05*

Club Náutico d'Addaia

Well-run little marina on the east side of Cala Molí; 100 moorings, water and power points, no fuel pumps. *Tel. 971 36 58 84*

INFORMATION

Town Hall in Es Mercadal, Tel. 971 37 50 02

SURROUNDING AREA

Arenal d'En Castell   (102/C2–3)

This is a flourishing modern holiday resort with one of the best beaches on the island – fine white sand, stretching for a good 500 metres, and shelving gently into the often crystal-clear waters. This is a good place to stay, so here are some hotels. The *Castell Playa Fiesta* is a real family hotel for people who like to aim high: facilities include sauna, pool, rooms with sea view, jacuzzi and a small children's play area *(265 rooms, Platja d'En Castell, 1 May to 15 Oct, Tel. 971 35 80 88, Fax 971 35 81 19, category 1)*. One bar in particular where it really gets going after sundown, with song and guitar music, is the *Es Can (Cala Corp, 5)[*which has been set up in a cleft in the rock.

Arenal de Son Saura   (102/C2)

Small holiday development with what is normally a clean white sand beach, half-moon shaped and about 100 m long. It has a modest but good enough restaurant. Sportsfans will be able to surf (surfboards for hire), dive and go water-skiing; there are plans for a marina. If you want to find somewhere quieter take the path near the sea (about 1.2 km) at the left end of the beach to the next little cove, the *Cala Pudent*; usually there will only be a few swimmers here and some anglers.

Cala Tortuga (103/D3)
Cove with sandy beach and good for swimming when the sea is calm.

Na Macaret (102/C3)
On the same inlet as Port d'Addaia the flourishing holiday resort of Na Macaret is at the exit from the fishing harbour on the mouth of *Cala Molí*, the smallest of the twin coves. This was the site of the third and final British invasion in 1798, and is now a popular departure point for deep-sea fishing. The beach is sheltered but tiny.

Son Parc (102/C2–3)
The island's first and – so far – only golf course is set among pine groves and part of an up-and-coming holiday resort. The reason this remains the only golf course is because a competing project in the immediate vicinity of the present Es Grau nature reserve came to a halt because of the vigorous protests of the local people. The compact 9-hole course, which opened in 1977, has mainly long, fast greens that are not unduly difficult and a gently undulating terrain. Expansion of the course to 18 holes is planned but this does depend on how well demand and accommodation sales in the holiday resort develop. The complex is open all year round and has facilities for tennis as well as golf; there is also a club house complete with showers, bar and restaurant. The lowest green fee is about Ptas 5000, half an hour's practice with a professional costs about Ptas 3000. Enquiries and reservation: *Urbanización Son Parc, Es Mercadal, Tel. 971 36 38 40, Fax 971 35 17 48.*

A vulture as symbolic figure

The usually solo creature is tracing wide easy circles high in the heavens – and now the Menorcan ornithologist focuses his binoculars to get a closer look. He can see a white body but this is certainly no gull since the trailing edges of the wings are of unbroken black. This is a real thrill for any birdwatcher since it means he has spotted one of the rare *alimoches*, the local Egyptian vultures. This small breed of vulture *(Neophron percnopterus)* lives singly, in pairs, or in small groups, in quiet places out in the countryside away from people, and on the cliffs of the north. Unusually, these Egyptian vultures, unlike their fellows elsewhere around the Mediterranean, do not migrate south for the winter. As a species they are not found anywhere else in the Balearics, but on Menorca they have gradually been elevated to the status of a kind of symbolic figure embodying untamed Nature and the spirit of the island.

The sunny side of the island

The longest beaches, the best-known bays and the largest hotels are on the south side of the island

His Highness Archduke Ludwig Salvator, who had an intimate knowledge of the Balearics and was already thinking on eco-friendly lines a hundred years ago, described the south of Menorca as rather an unhealthy place to live. The Habsburger was particularly uneasy about the *barrancs*, the gullies scoured out of the soft limestone by thousands of years of gushing rainfall. When it was hot these were, as he saw it, a source of "mephitic airs" – in other words, foul-smelling vapours – which "lend succour to malaria".

The original inhabitants of the island presumably thought otherwise. The land here is more fertile, and the climate more agreeable than on the north coast. It is precisely in and among the large *barrancs* in the southwest of Menorca that there is an immense number of prehistoric sites waiting to be excavated. There are up to 60 potential archaeological digs to every square kilometres, thus making

The idyllic bay of Cala Galdana

the island one of the richest concentrations of prehistoric sites in Europe. Among experts Menorca enjoys the reputation of being one "vast open-air museum".

Menorca's holidaymakers would presumably not go along with the Archduke's pithy pronouncements either, since this is where some of their favourite destinations are located: the idyllic Cala Galdana, the long beaches at Sant Tomás and Son Bou, and the quiet cove at Cala Trebalùger.

ALAIOR

(**104/B2-3**) There is an old chestnut that every single Menorcan will have heard, which is supposed to be about a trip by the mayor of Alaior to a meeting in distant Galicia. The story goes that this island innocent abroad was already booked into his hotel for the night before the start of the conference. Consequently, for the benefit of the night porter, the dignitary translated his request for a morning alarm call from his own local dialect into his best standard Spanish: "*Y mañana me gritan a las siete, por* *favor"* (*gritan* means "wake up" in Menorcan, but "shout at" in Spanish), whereupon the porter, mightily offended, replied "Sir, here no one would ever dream of shouting at any of our guests". They also say that the mayor overslept and missed the opening of the conference but did have a really good time during the rest of it.

On Menorca Alaior (pop. 6200) is also synonomous with cheese. The Coinga farming co-operative alone – maker, under the *Queso de Mahón* brand name, of Menorca's most famous cheese – can call on a herd of around 15,000 dairy cows, which, in their turn, are looked after by 170 fortunate dairy farmers. Another well-known local brand is *La Payesa*;

up until a few years ago the milk also went to make *La Menorquina*, a top quality make of ice cream which is popular throughout the Balearics, but the company has since transferred its operation to the mainland.

A brief look at the history of the place: founded in 1304, Alaior was soon making a name for itself as a thriving centre for producing cotton and woollen cloth. Many of the older buildings date from the 17th century. These include *Sant Diegu* (1623), the former Franciscan monastery, where a few families still live and work in the cells, the Town Hall (*Ajuntament*, 1612), and the massive Baroque parish church of *Santa Eulària*. On the road to the cemetery, at the northern exit from the town *(Camí del Cos)* in the direction of Fornells, they used to have horse racing up until a few years ago, but this fine custom has come to an end.

Adding the final touches to Menorca's world-famous cheese

SHOPPING

The market is *Thursday 9 am–1 pm (Avda. Huguet and C/. Comercio).*

Hand-made dolls are sold by *María Isabel de Salort (Plaça Generalísimo, 1).*

For excellent men's shoes, with a classical cut, there is *Timoner (C/. Comercio, 3)* and, also very elegant, the shoe-makers *Gomila Melia S.A. (C/. Miguel de Cervantes, 46).*

You can taste and buy cheese at *Coniga (C/. des Mercadal, 8)* or *La Payesa (Pons Martín, C/. Maó, 64).*

1 Cala Galdana
This ideal holiday beach, in a green oasis and sheltered by cliffs, is threatened by building mania (page 69)

2 Basílica de Son Bou
The most architecturally impressive example of

Menorca's early Christian basilicas (page 66)

3 Torre d'En Gaumés
A walled prehistoric settlement with water cisterns and storage chambers built around three *talaiots* and a *taula* precinct (page 66)

HOTELS

San Valentin
In this top hotel, only yards from the beach, you can expect four-star luxury – and prices to match. Comfortably appointed, pool, satellite TV. *214 rooms, Urbanzación Torre Solí Nou, Tel. 971 37 27 48, Fax 971 37 23 75, category 1*

Sol Milanos
What distinguishes this hotel is its all-round comfort and friendly service, especially for children, who are catered for by a kindergarten with its own programme. A pool, tennis courts, and an attractive garden complete the facilities. The beach is about 200 metres away. *300 rooms, Platja de Son Bou, Tel. 971 37 11 75, Fax 971 37 12 26, May–Oct, category 1*

Sol Pingüinos
With just on 300 rooms this establishment is already a real heavyweight among the island's hotels. Here too the Iberian hotel group has opted for quality, albeit at the expense of individuality. Besides all the features and mod cons of a three-star hotel there is also a garden with pool and tennis courts. As is often the case with the big hotels a complete package with a tour operator works out cheaper. *Platja de Son Bou, Tel. 971 37 10 75, Fax 971 37 12 26, May–Oct, category 1–2*

INFORMATION

Town Hall, Tel. 971 37 10 02

SURROUNDING AREA

Son Bou **(104/A2–3)**
At just on 3 km *Platges de Son Bou* has the longest sandy beach in Menorca. With its fine-grained golden sands, shelving gently into the sea, showers and toilets it is ideal for families. For children there is also a mini amusement park with waterslides in the adjoining *Sant Jaume Mediterrani* development.

Prehistoric settlement writ large at Torres d'en Gaumés

At the eastern end of the beach there seems to have been a small township in the 4th century and aerial photography shows a faint street pattern below the sea. All that can be seen of it now is what is left of the ★ *Basílica de Son Bou*. Rediscovered in 1951, this consists of the bases of two colonnades which divide the main building into a central nave with two narrower side-aisles, foundation walls and a big stone font with a trefoil-shaped basin. Built in the 5th century, this is the clearest example there is of the architectural form taken by Menorca's early Christian basilicas.

Torralba d'En Salort (104/C3)

This *talaiot* structure (which is not on the main road but on the smaller minor road from Alaior to Cala En Porter) has not been restored yet and is in a pretty poor condition. This is in sharp contrast to *Sa Taula de Torralba*

which is one of the best preserved stone circles of its kind on the island. Animal bones and a small bronze statue symbolizing a bull have been found in the area around the standing stones.

Torre d'En Gaumés (104/B3)

★ A turning 2.5 km along the Alaior–Son Bou road leads to one of the most extensive archaeological sites in the Balearics, where a particularly large number of finds have been made. Around 1400 B.C. there must have been a proper township here, as the clearly visible remains of rooms, walls, cisterns, and store-rooms testify, with at its centre the taula and the three *talaiots*. The most prominent features are the burial chamber (the oldest part of the complex), now known as *Ses Roques Llises*, and a large stone-roofed chamber, *Sa Camera de sa Garita*, which was probably used for storage or as an assembly hall.

FERRERÍES

(101/E4) Rust-red rocks, reddish brown fields and, close to the road, a new suburb that is anything but beautiful: at first sight Ferreríes (pop. 3500) does not appear to have much to recommend it. But first impressions can be misleading and the picturesque old quarter in the higher part of town – and especially the antique charm of the Carrer de Sa Font – more than make up for anything else.

The name of the place seems to imply iron and early ironworks (iron is *ferrum* in Latin), but the town only became important when Richard Kane, the island's much-respected British governor, ordered the building of the road between Mahón and Ciutadella, and Ferreríes became an active part of the island's trade network. A few years ago European institutions also came to the aid of the town, this time by supplying EU funding to help with agricultural diversification and to build up the market.

SHOPPING

Ferreríes weekly market – *Es Mercat (Sat 8 am–midday in summer, 9 am–1 pm in winter, Plaça Espanya)* – has become even more of an attraction since the European Union has helped out with schemes for speeding up farm-diversification. Hence you will also find a range of handicrafts as well as the usual fresh fruit and vegetables, meat, fish, and typical Menorcan specialities.

One thing you must try is the local delicacy *bunyols de fromatge*. These are little deep-fried doughnuts with a cheese filling which can be bought at bakeries in the old town.

Hort de Sant Patrici

This farm north of Ferreríes has its own farm shop where you can sample their wares before you buy. Their own farm products on sale include cheese, sausages, wine and fruit. You can also look round parts of the farm, and, from 10 to 11.30 on any weekday morning except Friday, you can also watch the farm produce being processed. *Camí Ruma, Tel. 971 37 37 02, sales 10 am–1 pm and 5–7 pm, closed Sat afternoon and Sun*

ACCOMMODATION

S'Atalaia (Tel. 971 37 42 32), one of the island's two official campsites, is on the road from *Ferreríes to Cala Galdana (km 4)*. It is about 3 km from the sea, and is well-run and well-appointed, with showers, a swimming pool and a little supermarket. The fact that the attitude of landowners to unofficial camping has hardened considerably in recent years should make this campsite all the more welcome so far as camping in general is concerned.

On the same road (fork right) you will find one of Menorca's three farms that also act as guest houses: *Son Triay Nou (4 rooms, Tel./Fax 971 15 50 78)*. Here you can spend your holiday on the farm; they have a swimming pool and a tennis court as well.

The *Club Escola Menorquina* puts on twice-weekly shows in summer by the best Spanish riding school *(Wed and Sun from 8.30 pm)*. Bookings and information: *Tel. 971 15 05 59.*

Town Hall. Tel. 971 37 30 03

Cala Mitjana   (101/D–E5)

You can get to this cove on foot by a path along the cliffs (about 1 km) or by car (left about 1.5 km before Cala Galdana). What greets you is a semicircular beach of fine white sand 100 m long and surrounded by pinewoods. Heading east, the road carries on to the lovely quiet *Cala Trebalùger* (about a 30-minute walk – which can be hard work in parts – from Cala Galdana). Unfortunately the landowner has closed off access to the cove by road, but, on the other hand, no one – and that includes the owner – can stop you approaching it from the sea (coming at it from this side you also have a beach 100 m wide).

A whole series of caves, prehistoric sites – and also the sources of many of the island's myths and legends – are to be found along the old watercourses that form the gullies which eventually lead into Cala Trebalùger. These *barrancs*, which in the course of thousands of years have dug their way as much as 50 m deep into the limestone, provide an environment – sheltered from the harsh *tramuntana* winds – for the "gardens of Menorca", with their own mild micro-climate. Without a proper guide, though, it is hard to get into them, especially since landowners are increasingly barring the way.

About halfway between Cala Galdana and Cala Sant Tomás there are two more coves: *Cala Fustam*, a little beach fringed with pinewoods and with a large cave at the left-hand end, and *Cala*

How stones become walls

Romantic natures like to reduce Menorca to "Wind and Stone". In fact both elements are closely intertwined here. The stone, which is basically nothing but a nuisance on the fields anyway, serves mainly as protection against the wind for the cultivated land. The layered drystone walls on Menorca are on average almost twice as high as those on the other Balearic islands where it is more a matter of defining the land boundaries. *Parets seques*, dry walls, are what they call the typical stone walls since they are built without using any mortar. There are projecting stones in places which serve as steps for getting over the wall. In 1988, after the skilled trade of the *pedrer*, the maker of stone walls, had almost died out in the Balearics, various schools began teaching it as a craft again. Nowadays a metre of *paret seca* costs about 50,000 to 80,000 pesetas.

Escorxada; because they are hard to get to they are both usually empty. The only way of getting there is to take a difficult road along the coast since the roads inland cross private estates which remain closed to the general public.

Cala Galdana (101/D5)

★ This beautiful bay would seem to have everything you need for your dream holiday. A green oasis, enclosed by dark-grey cliffs, it could originally only have been done justice with epithets such as "pictur-esque", "a proper paradise". Now, though, they are busy burying its charm under bricks and mortar, and the develop-ment of *Cala Galdana* is remorsely eating into the west-ern arm of the bay in particular with new apartments, holiday homes, restaurants and super-markets.

You get a good ∿ overall view of the bay by turning left at the first hotel on the way in. The beach is about 500 m long, and its fine golden sand makes it ideal for families. The waters inside the bay only get rough when, as rarely happens, the wind is from the south.

The *Grill Los Pinos (category 2)* restaurant, which has a good range of grills and fish dishes, has a pleasant terrace and is worth mentioning if only for its mag-nificent location on the offshore peninsula.

The best – and the cheapest – way to stay in one of Cala Gal-dana's many hotels is to sit down at home with the glossy brochures of the big package tour operators, and this applies

to almost everywhere on the coast. Just one suggestion at this point: for anyone who wants to take the whole family on holi-day, the self-catering flats and bungalows that are part of the three-star Cala Galdana holiday complex should be just right. The architecture may be second-rate but they are less than 150 m from the water, and they do have lovely gardens, a pool, fitness centre with jacuzzi, sauna, sunbathing facilities, etc. *(57 apartments, 204 rooms in the Hotel Cala Galdana, Tel. 971 37 30 00, Fax 971 37 30 26, open April–Nov, hotel and apartments caategory 2).*

If you are looking for some-where more out of the way in rural Menorca there is a place quite close to Cala Galdana where you can try their *agrotur-isme*, the Spanish version of a farm holiday. This is *Binisaid*, one of the island's early "alternative" forms of holiday accommo-dation. It is in a fabulous setting among the *barrancs*, surrounded by woods and just a few kilome-tres from the coast, and has its own access to idyllic bays, pool etc. *(Ctra. Ferreríes – Cala Galdana, km 4.3; information: Tel. 971 15 50 63).*

The *Escuela Náutica Cala Gal-dana (on the beach, Tel. 971 15 51 68, May–Oct)* caters for water sports for the entire family. Here the offspring can get expert tuition as well on how to wind-surf and waterski, there are courses on dinghy sailing and even a "ski-bus", an inflatable that looks like a kind of super sausage with handles that is towed by a motorboat; also rental of boards and boats.

ES MIGJORN GRAN

(101/F5) As places go on Menorca, this one is relatively young. It was founded for the second time in 1769 during the second British occupation. Since then little has changed apart from the name of the place, which used to be San Cristóbal. Amid the quiet little streets a few uniformly single-storey houses huddle round a simple church (begun in 1771) in the town centre. Only one local personality stands out from the town's otherwise uneventful history down the centuries. Francesc Camps was a doctor by profession but he found his true vocation in archaeology and local history. By writing down the island's songs and legends, and researching its customs and traditions, he was thus able to help Menorca's younger generation in particular to establish those roots that they so badly need if they are to withstand the onslaught, year upon year, of just on a million holidaymakers and the alien cultures that they bring with them. Sadly this local hero's birthplace and library are not currently open to the public.

RESTAURANTS

Ca'na Pilar
Another a good suggestion for the summer. The patio has that country-life feeling but combined with good plain Menorcan fare and only a few concessions to international tastes. *Ctra. Es Migjorn Gran – Es Mercadal, on the way out of town, no telephone, category 2–3*

S'Engolidor
Traditional and quite filling Menorcan cuisine at reasonable prices. Here, for example, you can try pork chops à la Menorquin or stingray with capers. In summer you can also dine outdoors on the terrace. *C/. Major, 3, Tel. 971 37 01 93, category 3*

ACCOMMODATION

If you decide to stay on in Migjorn ask about a room in *S'Engolidor*, the restaurant just mentioned. Their four rooms are plain but pleasant and you can also be treated like one of the family if you wish *(May–Oct)*.

INFORMATION

Town Hall, Tel. 971 37 00 75

SURROUNDING AREA

Cova d'es Coloms   (101/E–F5)
Because of its grandeur of scale the locals call this cave "the cathedral". At 24 m high, 11 m deep, and 16 m wide, it is one of Menorca's most impressive underground features. According to new research it was already being used as a temple in the pre-Christian era. There is an old Menorcan superstition that couples who enter the cave together will split up soon after; on the other hand, single people who meet with one another in the cave will be joined together by the power of fate.

The road from Es Migjorn Gran to Sant Tomás beach passes three archaeological sites. The *Talaiot de Binicodrell* close to the town has so far not been excavated, but there are plans for its restoration. The prehistoric settlement of *Sant Agustí Vell* is famous for a large roofed stone construction that led earlier archaeologists to the (mistaken) conclusion that the *taulas* were also simply the central pillar which supported a roof made of slabs. The third settlement, *Santa Mónica*, is interesting because here a row of *navetas* (predecessors of the *talaiots*) have been joined to a settlement that clearly was not a burial site but a place where people had their dwellings.

Platja Sant Tomás   (101/F5-6)

The road from Es Migjorn Gran to the sea takes you to three beaches which are only separated from one another by narrow tongues of rock. These are *Binigaus* in the west, and *Sant Adeodat* and *Sant Tomás* in the east. The latter two are more lively, and this is even more so for Platja Sant Tomás which has hotels and a holiday complex. Directly above the beach at Sant Adeodat there is a little bar where you can also get simple meals, with a fantastic sea view that goes well with a snack in the early evening. The *Sol Cóndores* at Sant Tom s has all the qualities you would expect of the Sol hotel chain: clean, modern and comfortable accommodation, surrounded by lush gardens and right on the sea *(three stars, 188 rooms, Platja Sant Tomás, Tel. 971 37 00 50, Fax 971 37 03 48, open April–Nov, category 2).*

To get to Binigaus, the quieter of the three beaches, there is a footpath right by the sea (about 1.2 km) or you can get there by car on a rather poor road that forks left about 2 km beyond Es Migjorn Gran. Its beach of fine, pale grey sand is particularly worth the effort in the high season when the other two beaches get packed out.

Not so much a dream, more a nightmare

It took just 25 gruelling minutes before the dream cove they had all raved about came into view. The approach was over bumpy roads and we nearly got lost several times, but, luckily, on Menorca all roads lead to the sea sooner or later.

This cove had already been warmly recommended to us as being "picturesque", "unspoilt", and so on. And "a proper paradise" gushed the guidebook. But in reality it looked very different. A film of sun-oil coated the brilliant blue waters, and plastic bags bobbed up and down in the sea close to the beach. As for the beach itself, this was absolutely jam-packed with bodies with barely an inch of space to spare, and, to cap it all, a stall on the sands was blaring out a mixture of salsa and the Spanish top of the pops through its P.A. system.

There are coves and beaches all over Menorca that are a dream and an idyll. It is just that at the height of the summer they are anything but! And you may even have to pay simply for parking there. So, in the peak holiday season, the best advice is stick to the local beach that you already know, and that way you won't be disappointed.

71

Menorca's Mediterranean soul

Soft shades of gold and amber, weathered façades, paved alleys, pastel palaces in the old town

In Ciutadella all is still right with the world. This is not because, as you might think at first sight, that time had lost its way somewhere between the late Middle Ages and the present. On the contrary: it is because, behind the serene old façades of the houses and palaces, society here is well integrated and well organized. Unemployment is minimal, many of the people who live here work in the leather business, commerce and tourism, the crime rate is exceptionally low, and the quality of life ranks with the best in Spain.

Exports of wool and leather and thriving commerce must already have played an important role in the town of the Middle Ages and laid the foundations for the "traditional and stately" Ciutadella always referred to by the island chroniclers with a healthy dose of respect. Until the 18th century Ciutadella was able to assert itself as the capital of Menorca. And the island's Bishop has to this day retained his allegiance to the "National

Plaça d'es Born in Ciutadella

Historic Monument" as the whole of the inner city – which is still the seat of his bishopric – has recently been designated.

What is new, though, is the rise of the big holiday resorts that surround Ciutadella. These include Cala En Forcat in the west, particularly popular with the British, Cala Morell in the north, known for its luxury holiday properties, and, in the south, Cala Blanca and Son Xoriguer which are both constantly expanding.

CALA BLANCA

(100/B4) The name refers both to a holiday resort – with nothing special to distinguish it from other similar places on the island – and to the bay on the southern edge of the town which owes its name ("White Bay") to the gleaming white sand, framed by a little grove of pines in the background. The cliffs to the left and the right of the beach have restaurants and bars which excel not so much for the quality of the food as for their wonderful location. Here a ☘ view of romantic Menorcan sunsets is pretty well guaranteed for most evenings. There are waterslides for children too. The *Cova de Parella*, not far from the bay, is famous for its wealth of stalactites and stalagmites and a small subterranean lake. There were plans for an English company to open it up for tourism but fortunately it appears that this project is currently not being followed up.

INFORMATION

Tourist information centre in Ciutadella

SURROUNDING AREA

Cala En Bosc (100/B5)
Cala En Bosc is the next holiday resort along from the development on the cape at Cap d'Artrutx. Here too the architecture is pretty average, more for use than ornament, plus an offshore beach, fine white sand, and often clear seawater. A little train on rubber wheels with three or four carriages – the *Minitren* – runs round the entire bay between Cap d'Artrutx and Son Xoriguer.

Boats and yachts can be hired from *CSS (Tel. 971 35 01 74)*; they also give sailing lessons and run training courses for the various sailing proficiency certificates. Information from: *Tel. 908 63 66 29 (mobile)*.

Cala Parejals (100/B5)
This is particularly popular with Sunday anglers from Ciutadella who come here to fish. Divers also take full advantage of the diversity of its underwater world. The way here is along a coastal path from the *Platja de Son Xoriguer*.

Cala Santandría (100/B4)
A pioneer centre of Menorca's still relatively young tourist industry. Lots of bare rock, lots of

MARCO POLO SELECTION: CIUTADELLA AND THE WEST

1 Ciutadella
Certainly the loveliest of all the island's towns: venerable, historic and stately, clean too, and a good place to explore on foot (page 76)

2 Cala En Turqueta
The quintessential dream cove: gently sloping sandy beach, shady pines, smooth rounded rocks (page 84)

3 Cala Macarella
Crystal clear, bright blue water, ringed round by greenery and grey cliffs – Menorca's vision of paradise (page 84)

4 Nau d'es Tudons
Built 3400 years ago from massive blocks of sandstone, this is the oldest roofed building in Europe (page 84)

buildings, hotel, bars, villas, restaurants – and not much greenery. The beach is white and coarse-grained. An old British peel tower (18th century) guards the entrance to the bay. A particularly interesting feature is the cave/home/studio which local sculptor Nicolau Cabrisas has spent many years transforming into his own personal vision of reality; the walls of his abode are covered with masks, faces and figures.

The *Poseidón* is a friendly little hotel, with a family atmosphere, that has the added advantage of being right on the beach *(13 rooms, Tel. 971 38 26 44, Fax 971 48 27 04, category 2)*. Also right next to the sea – it is actually in one of the caves – is the *Sa Nacra* restaurant, which has an international menu but specializes in paella *(Urbanización Sa Caleta, near Hotel Price, Tel. 971 38 62 06, open May to Oct, category 2)*.

CALA MORELL

(100/C2) *Son Morell* and *Marina* are two places that have grown together to become one of the really big holiday resorts in the north of Menorca. Particularly in the spring and the autumn, when there is hardly a soul around to bring the development to life, the white houses on the slopes of the weatherbeaten russet rocks of the *Cala Morell* cove look quite out of place. The architecture of the complex is reminiscent of Ibiza, with a few of the details that are typical of Menorca such as the imaginatively positioned drain-pipes that help to soften the rather harsh aspect of so many walls.

Thousands of years ago, halfway between sea and sky, the early inhabitants of Menorca used a little side-arm of the bay to make themselves dwellings in the soft limestone. The caves – there are just 20 of them – were made habitable around 900 B.C., and some of them have niches and central supporting columns. They are easily accessible from the road. Limestone above, red sandstone below – this is the start of the imaginary line devised by the geologists to separate the much older Tramuntana in the north of the island from the Migjorn in the south. The line runs between Cala Morell and Mahón. The small stony beach has little to recommend it.

ACCOMMODATION

Biniatram
Farm holiday accommodation, known here as *agroturisme*. Swimming pool available. *4 rooms, Camino de Algaiarens, turn right before Son Morell, km 1, Tel. 971 38 31 13*

INFORMATION

Tourist information centre in Ciutadella

SURROUNDING AREA

Cala Algaiarens   (100/C2)
These are two lovely quiet coves but they have been hitting the headlines since 1992. They lie within the boundaries of a very big estate and the landowner, Ricardo Squella, was one of the first to levy a charge for using the road to the beach "to cover the cost of cleaning up the area after

the season ended, and to pay for putting in and maintaining a car park". Protests from the local population were not long in coming since for generations they had been accustomed to using the coves – now part of the nature conservation area – not just for swimming but for camping as well. Squella later relented sufficiently to give free passage for residents of Ciutadella, where he owns the Palacio Squella, but refused to allow the same concession for anyone else. The beach itself is divided in two by a line of rocks. Its eastern section borders on a small freshwater lagoon. This is fed by the winter rainfall that is chanelled through the *La Vall* gulley and runs into the sea here.

Cala Ses Fontanelles   (100/C2)

The beach here shelves more steeply than at Cala Algaiarens and is mainly used by people from the boats that anchor off the rocks. The overland route forks left about 1 km before the road gets to Cala Algaiarens.

CIUTADELLA

☛City Map inside back cover
(100/B3) ★Although Ciutadella, with a population of 21,000, is only slightly smaller than Mahón, its rhythm of life appears to be more relaxed. The people here seem to have more time than those at the busier eastern end of the island. Everyday life proceeds at a more even – and perhaps more human – pace. Here the barber, with his folding chair and beach sandals, still ventures out to warm himself for a bit in the setting sun in

front of his shop when he has run out of beards. Here they often still greet strangers in town with a brief nod of the head, and here the older folk still have plenty to say for themselves, in thick clouds of cigar smoke and conducting a lively *tertulia* in the *Cercle Artistic*, or in the shadow of the obelisk that, like a warning finger over the Plaça d'es Born, serves as a reminder of when Turkish pirates almost completely destroyed the place. Following that bloody assault, which was well over four hundred years ago, 3000 people were carried off into slavery, and the city was so thoroughly plundered and ravaged that they had to start from nothing again and rebuild it.

In the mornings the shadow of the obelisk that stands on the *Plaça d'es Born* and commemorates the *Any de sa Desgràcia*, the "year of the disaster", points to the *Ajuntament (Town Hall)*. At one time a Moorish fortress, then the castle of King Alfonso III, who liberated the town and the island from the Moors, it was later the residence of a line of island governors. The present building dates from the 19th century and houses the town council. Every year, on 9 July, the "record of the terror" is opened and read aloud. It tells of the 15,000 Turkish "unbelievers" who besieged the town in 1558. It also tells of the nobles and the heroes of Ciutadella who for seven bloody days defied their superior numbers.

Ciutadella Cathedral

On the right of the town hall a ⬧ *mirador (viewing platform)* rises above the city wall and affords a panoramic view over the whole of the port.

In the afternoons the shadow of the obelisk falls on the façades of the eastern flank of the Plaça d'es Born. A row of cafés, souvenir shops and restaurants lines the ground floor of the palaces – *Palau Torresaura, Palau Vivó* and *Palau Salort*, all in *marés*, the lovely honey-coloured sandstone which in earlier centuries acted as air conditioning thanks to its ability to "breathe". The only one open to the public is the Palau Salort, parts of which are on view. The façade of the Palau Vivó next door has a very English look about it.

Buildings on the north side of the square include the *Cercle Artìstic* – founded in 1881 and completely renovated in the early 1990s – and the *Teatre Municipal d'es Born*, the municipal theatre, which has also been fully restored. In the "Artistic Circle", though, the talk is not so much about art, but they do love to get involved in the politics of the day and the latest local scandal, all voicing their own opinions and often at full volume. The theatre next door screens films, puts on plays and stages the occasional musical event. Opposite is the head post office, a few bars, and the chapel of *Sant Francesc* (completed in 1627), which was built on the site of an older church that was destroyed by the pirates.

Along the *Carrer Major d'es Born* you come to the *cathedral* on the *Plaça de la Catedral*. It owes much of its imposing square-cut appearance to the reinforcement work that had to be carried out when part of the dome collapsed in 1628. In 1795 a papal edict elevated this reconstruction to the status of the island's Cathedral – a decision roundly criticized by Mahón. The present clock tower dates back to the minaret of a mosque which dominated the square until the 13th century *(viewing daily 9 am–1 pm and 6–9 pm)*. There are a number of anecdotes and legends about the cathedral. They say that when it was being rebuilt they had to cover up the window openings because hundreds of birds were flocking into the church when the priest was at prayer. In the course of its history the cathedral has also served as sanctuary for many of those who had fallen out of favour with one or other of the island's governors.

The *Palau Olivar* opposite the front of the cathedral marks what was once the start of the *Judería*, the town's Jewish quarter *(Carrer Palau, Carrer Sant Jeroni* and *Carrer Sant Francesc)*, with a row of more modest mansion houses.

Opposite the right-hand side entrance of the cathedral *(Porta de la Llum,* door of light) the *Carrer del Roser* branches off to the south. After fifty paces you come across the narrow façade of the *Esglèsia del Roser* (begun in the 12th century), which nowadays only opens up for musical events and exhibitions (information from the tourist information centre on the Plaça de la Catedral). At the end of the alley stands the mansion of one of the most influential families on the island, the *Palau Saura* (17th century), which is reckoned to be among the most magnificent of Ciutadella's palaces. On the left, via the *Carrer Santíssim,* the (17th-century) *Palau Martorell* – or *Cas Duc,* "duke's house" as the

Menorcans like to call it – comes into view. This palace in the old town has its own lovely adjoining garden, but sadly this is not on public view. Peace reigns on the quiet *Carrer del Portal d'Artrutx* and *Carrer del Castell de Rupit* until you get to the *Mercat,* the covered market, where everything comes back to life again. In the white and dark-green tiled hall each trade has its own side of the building. Facing the butchers, on the other side of the *Carrer de la Palma,* there is a row of vegetable stalls and traditional market bars where there is always plenty going on. In the *Carrer del Socors* there is the sound of voices as from time to time snatches of music penetrate the thick walls of the *Esglèsia del Socors.* The

Ciutadella's peaceful port reflects its relaxed life-style

Augustinian monastery here was founded in 1648 and then converted in the 20th century to serve as an academy for the training of young musicians *(Capella Davídica)*; its alumni include the international baritone Joan Pons.

On the right the name of Saura crops up again, this time with reference to a palace with a plainer façade which was built in the 18th century, then destroyed and finally resurrected with the help of the English. A little further along you pass by the *Capella del Sant Crist* (begun in 1667) on the way back to the central pedestrian precinct. The small domed chapel was a particular favourite of the sheep shearers who in the Middle Ages provided the wool that was the port of Ciutadella's most important export.

Lining the *Carrer Josep M. Quadrado* are its beautiful Moorish arcades, *Ses Voltes*. Here Ciutadella is getting commercial again: businesses, bakers, shoes, books, a hairdresser – retailers and small tradesmen flourish in the shadow of these lovely arches, each one of them different from the others. The bars on the adjoining *Plaça Nova* are usually quite packed, mainly with newcomers to the town who welcome this chance to stop for a while and enjoy a quick drink or a glass of lemonade. Straight ahead now comes the *Plaça Alfons III or Plaça de Ses Palmeres*, as the townsfolk call it, which leads to the *Camí de Maó*, the road that runs across the island to the east coast.

Heading west, back in the opposite direction, you have the *Sant Antoni* which becomes the *Carrer Sant Josep*. Here you find a number of ☙ restaurants and cafeterias that are mainly frequented by the locals. On the right, at the end of the *Carrer Santa Clara*, is another palace, that of the Barons of Lluriach *(Castell Lluriach)*, the first members of Menorca's nobility, who were installed here by Charles II after the battle against the occupying Moors on Spain's south coast. Further north on the left is the *Bastió de Sa Font*, the bastion which is all that remains of the city walls that up until 1869 protected Ciutadella's old town; the ring road that begins on the right duplicates the line of the old walls in tarmac.

But back to the narrow lanes of the inner city. Another palace, *Can Sequella* (17th century), and the *Bishop's Palace, (Palau Episcopal*, also 17th century), lie on the edge of the *Carrer Sant Sebastiá* and the *Carrer del Bisbe* (with a superb old bakery). The *Carrer d'es Mirador* finally brings you back to where the tour started, on the *Plaça d'es Born* by the municipal theatre. On the right you can see the steps that lead down to the sea. Little souvenir stands on the left and boutiques and shops on the right follow their passage down to the *Café Balear*. As the *Café Bosch* is to Palma de Mallorca, so the *Café Balear* is to Ciutadella: this is where it all happens, the place for a chat and taking a quick look, the place to meet for afternoon coffee, which passes as a "restaurant" for holidaymakers who just want to eat a few potato crisps, the *taas* bar with a view of the town hall, the city wall covered in capers, and the serene waters of the harbour, in short: an "institution" that is popular with visitors and locals alike. Since the end of 1993 the business has been fully computerized (with the owner's daughter at the keyboard). Each Coca Cola is totted up electronically, though this does not necessarily mean that there are no holdups. Incidentally, the *Café Balear* on the Cala En Bosc is a new venture by the same proprietor.

MUSEUMS

Bastió de Sa Font (U/A2)
Exhibits from the Middle Ages and the time of the Moorish occupation, historic documents and texts. *C/. Portal de Sa Font, open daily except Sun/Mon 10 am–1 pm and 7–9 pm*

Castell de Sant Nicolau (U/C6)
Small local history museum with old photographs, mementos of notable personalities etc. *Passeig Marítim, open daily except Sun 7–9 pm*

Palau Salort (U/B3)
The only palace in Ciutadella that is open to the public; on view are salons, bedchambers, smoking room, plus bathroom, kitchen and garage; decorating the *patio* is a 1920s Buick. There is a bar in the palace. *Plaça d'es Born, 1 May – 30 Oct, open daily except Sun 9.30 am–1.30 pm*

RESTAURANTS

Ca's Quintu (U/B1)
Classic island fare and very good selection of *tapas*. *Plaça Alfons III, Tel. 971 38 10 02, category 2*

The same owner also has the *Club Nautic* restaurant in the port

La Guitarra (U/B3)
According to Roberto, the owner, this is the place for local home-cooking, and with his mother in the kitchen that certainly seems to be the case; meat dishes figure most prominently on the menu. *C/. Dolores, 1, Tel. 971 38 13 55, open daily except Sun, category 1–2*

A whole line of restaurants stretches along the *waterfront* in the port. These are mostly patronized by holidaymakers and standards can vary. Here are some of the better ones:

El Bribón (U/B3)
This specializes in fish and seafood. *C/. Marina, Tel. 971 38 50 50, category 2*

Casa Manolo (U/B3)
Probably the best-known of the waterfront restaurants. Its speciality is fish from the grill. *C/. Marina, Tel. 971 38 00 03, category 2*

Sa Figuera (U/B3)
Specialities are meat dishes and pickled fish. *C/. Marina, Tel. 971 38 21 12, category 2*

Forn de Ca'n Leo (U/B2)
Not a restaurant but a bakery with all kinds of goodies featuring cheese and pastry to fill that gap. *C/. Alaior, 44, no table reservations*

SHOPPING

Rosa Botella Playa (U/B3)
Individually crafted fashion jewellery and accessories. *Plaça d'es Born, 28*

Casa Coll (U/B1)
Here you can get all kinds of cakes, pastries and confectionery at acceptable prices. *C/. de Maó, 8*

Casa Fayas (U / B2)
A good selection of Menorca cheese, *sobrasadas* and other farm products typical of the island. *Murada d'Artrutx, 28*

JAP – Artículos típicos (U / B3)
Typical Menorcan souvenirs, especially leather goods, in an attractive little shop close to the port. *Baixada Capelloch, 12*

Patricia Mesquida y García (O)
Nothing but leather. *Ronda Baleares, 9.* Has a factory outlet as well, with the emphasis on clothing, belts, bags, shoes, on the road heading south. *Ctra. de Santandría*

Pastisseria Ca'n Moll (U / B2)
Cakes and confectionery made following their own – often quite idiosyncratic – recipes. *C/. Roser, 1*

Tocinería Miguel Román (U / B–C2)
Sausages, *sobrasadas* and pasties they have made themselves. *C/. Don Sacio, 26*

Top Leather Factories (U / B1)
Leatherwear at reasonable prices and in a broad range: shoes, coats, trousers, bags. *Ctra. de Maó, 194, and in the old town, C/. de Ses Moreres, 33*

HOTELS

Ciutadella (U / B1–2)
Simple "Hostal-Residencia" right in the centre, many rooms with bath; quite a good restaurant. *17 rooms, C/. Sant Eloi, 10, Tel./Fax 971 38 34 62, open all year, category 2–3*

Esmeralda (U / B6)
Three-star hotel, well-run, no frills, right by the harbour mouth with view of the sea and the lighthouse. Garden with swimming pool, tennis court and kindergarten. Lots of foreign guests. *158 rooms, Passeig Sant Nicolau, 171, Tel. 971 38 02 50, Fax 971 38 02 58, open April–Oct, category 1–2*

Menurka (U / B1)
♫ This hostel – open to allcomers – is near the centre. It is quite simple but modern and clean, and is probably the cheapest place to stay in Ciutadella itself. *21 rooms, C/. Domingo Sabio, 6, Tel. 971 38 14 15, Fax 971 38 12 82, category 2–3*

SPORT

Sailing (U / A–B4)
You can hire boats of every class, from dinghies to yachts, from *Yacht Brokerage, Port de Ciutadella, Tel. 971 48 20 44*, and from *Sports Massanet, Motonáutica, C/. Lepanto, Tel. 971 48 21 86.*

Diving (U / B3)
The western end of Menorca has plenty of diving centres as well as a wonderfully diverse underwater world. Information from *Sports Massanet, Motonáutica, C/. Marina, 66, Tel. 971 48 21 86.*

Tennis (O)
There are public tennis courts with floodlighting at the *Club de Tenis Ciutadella*, in the *Tòrre del Ram* district, *Tel. 971 38 20 68.*

VIU Menorca (O)
This is the name of an association of "alternative" guides to Menorca who, since 1994, have been organizing unusual but consistently eco-friendly ways of exploring the island. These include excursions by boat, walks, bird-watching, pony-trekking, cycling tours, etc. Information:

C/. Ramón Llull, 9, Tel. 971 38 37 08.

The hotspots of nightlife in Ciutadella are the bars that open up in the evening around *Es Plá de Sant Joan*, the square at the landward end of the port where, in the shade of the boatsheds, the fishermen always used to beach their *llauts* to give them a fresh coat of paint. Now the scene is one of neon lights, hard drinking and lots of flash posers, not necessarily to everyone's liking.

One of the really big discos in the west of the island, which looks good, with lots of lighting and special effects, and has mixed music, mixed punters and a programme of live events in the summer is *Adagio's* in the *Son Oleo* district. The *Ali Baba (C/. Marina, 27)*, which is also open to allcomers, is one of the take off points for Menorca by night. A small disco with plenty of atmosphere, especially at the weekend is the ✝ ✪ *Disco 1800* which is in the heart of town opposite the cathedral. The ✝ *Es Glop (Passeig de Sant Joan)* is a music bar with a terrace and a cool ambience which is popular with the young.

The *Club Mannix (Avda. del Mar, after midnight)*, with its Latin American sounds and exclusive atmosphere, is the haunt of well-to-do Menorcan men on the lookout for unshockable – or unwary – female visitors to the island. Although open in the afternoons the ✪ *Es Molí d'es Compte (Plaça Alfons III)* only really gets going at night.

Oficina de Información turística
Plaça de la Catedral, Tel. 971 38 26 93 (open May–Oct)

Bus stop for the service to Mahón: *C/. Barcelona, 8.* Buses run there several times a day but how often depends very much on the time of year. Information via *Tel. 971 36 03 61* (in Spanish) or from tourist information.

Lines also run from Ciutadella to Cala Santandría, Cala Blanca, Los Tronquilos and Cala En Bosc, and also to Cala En Blanes, Cala En Bruch, Los Delfines and Cala En Forcat.

– Town Hall: *Tel. 971 38 10 50*
– Car rental: *Europcar, C/. Conquistador, 59, Tel. 971 38 29 98*
– Head post office: *Plaça d'es Born, 5*
– Taxi call centre: *Tel. 971 38 23 35 and Tel. 971 38 11 97*

Island cruises with Líneas de la Cruz go to a number of remote beaches and coves that are often nearly impossible to get to by car or on foot. The company also operates some glass-bottomed boats that take in almost the entire coastline. Day cruises run from Ciutadella to the north-west via *Cala Morell* to *Cala del Pilar* and to the south-west via *Cala En Bosc* and *Arenal de Son Saura* to *Cala Galdana*; in summer these include stopping off for a swim. In the summer months the boats put out to sea *daily at 10 am*, and get back at around *5 pm*. They leave Ciutadella from the embarkation quay in the port. Ticket sales: *Es Port Shop, Tel. 971 48 17 90.*

Arenal de Son Saura (100/C5)

✪ This bay has two beaches that are separated by a small tongue of land. They have fine white sand, are sheltered from the wind, and fringed with pines, making them the ideal place for spending a day on the beach. A word of warning, though: occasionally currents can build up in the bay that are capable of sweeping you out to sea.

To get here from Ciutadella take the Camí de Sant Joan de Missa by the white country church of the same name and at Son Vivó turn right past the old square tower of Torre Saura Vell.

Son Saura has become a particular favourite with the Ciutadellans. If the long sandy beach is already full it is worth heading east on foot. After scrambling over the rocks of *Punta d'es Governador* (about 500 m)

you reach the next cove, the considerably smaller *Cala d'es Talaier*. The sand here is ochre in colour, and it also has a backdrop of pines if you want shade from the sun.

Cala d'es Degollador (100/B3)

This inlet some 500 m south of the entrance to Ciutadella harbour owes its bloodcurdling name ("Cut–throat's Cove") not, as you might think, to the shady characters selling cans of drink on the beach, but to an attack by pirates which is supposed to have encountered its first resistance here. The little beach is mainly used by the residents of Ciutadella who come here for a swim.

Cala En Forcat (100/A3)

West of Ciutadella there is a whole holiday town which has sprung up from the rocks of the coast. The developments at *Cala En Blanes, Cala En Forcat* and *Cala En Brut* have dovetailed so thoroughly with *Los Delfines* that in places it is hard to see where one

Just one of the beautiful coves on the south coast: Arenal de Son Saura

ends and the other begins. The whole sector is given over to tourism and the tourists. These are mostly English and they stay in the relatively cheap family hotels and the blocks of holiday flats that are everywhere. The coastline is also dotted with a number of villas with fabulous views of the sea.

Each of the bays has at least one little beach. The largest is probably *Cala En Blanes* which is about 50 m wide, but anyone expecting to come upon a broad expanse of deserted beach here is doomed to disappointment. What is quite spectacular is the sight of the saltwater geysers. These *bufadors* spout small jets up into the air on the western edge of Cala En Forcat. They are not caused by volcanic activity, however, but result from a system of caves and pipes that reacts to water pressure. In earlier days the citizens of Ciutadella used to go fishing from the rocks of the *Cales Piques* further to the north – here it is Cales (plural) as opposed to Cala (singular) because there are two narrow coves reaching deep into the rocks. Nowadays holidaymakers in *Los Delfines* use the tiny little patches of sand for swimming in the relatively deep water of the coves.

A suggested hotel: the *Almirante Farragut*, a good three-star hotel near the top of the middle-range, with sterling service and comfortable rooms *(472 rooms, Tel. 971 38 28 00, Fax 971 38 20 00, open May–Oct, category 1–2)*.

Cala Macarella (101/D5)

★ Crystal clear, turquoise waters, ringed by overgrown cliffs of grey limestone that form the background to an idyllic beach and a small biotype that once held tor-

toises and other wildlife – this is Menorca's vision of paradise. This paradise was under threat, though, from plans to develop the bay into a holiday resort, and the project was only halted because of outraged protests by the local population. Since 1992, the whole of the coastal strip between *Platja de Son Xoriguer* and *Biniali* – with very few exceptions – has been a nature conservation area and designated site of natural beauty, and currently the only facility that caters for the refreshment needs of those using the beach is a snackbar discreetly hidden away among the pines. There are also charges for using the car park that was established here in 1994. The cliffs along the shore hold several prehistoric grottos.

Cala En Turqueta (100/C5)

★ Along with Cala Macarella this has come to be featured as one of the archetypal "dream coves" of southern Menorca. To get here from Ciutadella take the Camí de Sant Joan de Missa and turn left at Son Vivó. The road forks after around 5 km: the left fork goes to Cala Macarella and the right fork to Cala En Turqueta. Car parking has to be paid for here too.

Nau d'es Tudons (100/C3)

★ The most famous prehistoric burial chamber on the island and probably the oldest known roofed building in Europe; this massive structure of sandstone slabs is reckoned to date back to about 3400 years ago. When restoration began in 1959 the excavation team found some bronze ornaments and the remains of human bones, which suggested that this was a (plundered) burial chamber. The inner chamber of the *nau* (*naveta* in Spanish) is divided into two storeys.

There is a legend surrounding this place. Long before it rained on the island the story goes that two Titans were fighting over a lady's affections. It was agreed that, as proof of their love, one of them would build a two-storey tower and the other would dig a well until it reached a depth where it struck water. The water flowed first, and this so enraged the other Titan that he wrenched a mighty stone from his tower (the present entrance hole) and hurled it at his rival. This had tragic consequences: the villain of the piece drowned himself in the well, while the lady died of a broken heart and was laid to rest in the Nau d'es Tudons. Incidentally, the deep well still exists today and goes by the name of the *Pou de Sa Barrina*.

Punta Nati   (100/B2)

☙ Most of the year all there is to be seen on the point is the occasional sheep searching out the weeds that sprout here and there from the crevices in the jumble of rocks. But come the spring the citizens of Ciutadella also pick their way along the bumpy road (*Avda. Francesc B. Moll*) that leads to the point, past the town's smoking rubbish dump and its everpresent flock of gulls. What they are looking for are the capers that grow in the shade of the stone walls. Pickled in brine for a couple of weeks these tender buds then mature into one of Menorca's real delicacies.

The lighthouse on this desolate cape has stood on this spot since 1913. From here you have a fantastic view out to sea and of the south-western coastline and two bays in the east, the *Cala Es Pous* and the *Cala Es Morts* ("bay of the dead"). This owes its name to an event in the winter of 1910 when a French passenger vessel, the "Général Chanzy", foundered on the rocks one stormy night and sank off the bay in a matter of seconds. All the 150 passengers and crew members were drowned apart from one young Frenchman: a cross and the broken and rusting skeleton of the shipwreck are still there today to tell the story.

Son Catlar   (100/C4)

This is the largest area of prehistoric settlement in the Balearics. To get there take the same road as from Ciutadella to Arenal de Son Saura (described earlier) then, before you get to the tower of *Torre Saura Vell*, you will find it on your left. It is scattered over more than 6 ha and is encircled by a partly ruined wall that runs for almost a kilometre. Within the wall there are cisterns, the foundations of living quarters, five stone towers (*talaiots*) and the central sacred precinct, the *taula*. All this has yet to be properly excavated and its age is unknown. What is certain is that there were people living here up until the end of the Roman occupation.

Torre Llafuda   (100–101/C–D3)

In its present overgrown state this large prehistoric settlement, competing as it does with the oak grove growing in and around it, has a magical, almost spooky, air about it. Submerged in the green shade here too you will find rooms, chambers, artificial caves, cisterns, a *talaiot* and a *taula*. Access: take the road from Ciutadella to Mahón, turn right at km 37, and then it is another 250 m or so.

Cutting across country and history

These routes are marked in green on the map on the inside front cover and in the Road Atlas beginning on page 100

① CONSERVATION AND NATURAL BEAUTY

A tour round the eastern part of the island where the landscape still retains its natural beauty; almost the entire route runs through nature conservation areas. 1 day, roughly 70 km

Your day's drive starts out from *Mahón*. The Mediterranean version of breakfast takes the form of fresh croissants and steaming *Café amb llet* and you can get this, or a full English breakfast, in the *Café Europa*, which is on the Rovellada de Dalt, not far from the Plaça de S'Esplanada. From here take the Avinguda Josep Maria Quadrado which will bring you to the Carretera de Ciutadella. At the next roundabout take the less busy Ronda de Sant Joan which goes off to the right and then on the left becomes the road to Fornells. At this point the countryside is already becoming quieter, greener and more peaceful.

All the roads on the right eventually lead to the sea; the one to Es Grau is signposted. After about 3 km you can see *Shangri-La*, the abortive holiday development which borders the southern section of *Albufera d'Es Grau*. This is the area that was marked out in the deeds drawn up by Unesco in October 1993 when it was designated the heartland of Menorca's biosphere reserve: 67 ha of wetlands, an eco-system where no human incursion is permitted, now or in the future. This is the home of wildfowl, geese, and herons, but also of rarer birds such as the osprey and the great white egret. And with the swarms of mosquito larvae and other insects there is plenty for them to feed on.

You drive back to the main road and then carry on in the direction of Fornells. About 2–3 km after the Ermita de Favàritx the road to *Cap de Favàritx* turns off to the right. At first the narrow asphalt road runs between fields and lush greenery but then with every kilometre the scenery becomes bleaker and more sombre. And the bushes by the roadside hug the ground ever more closely, until, at a certain point, there is nothing to be seen but dark rock. All that stands out from this bare, almost forbidding landscape is the lonely lighthouse at Favàritx. You can park at S'Escala on the bay opposite the lighthouse. If the sea is calm and you want to stop for a swim there are two small sandy coves close by, namely, *Cala Presili* and the somewhat larger *Cala Tòrtuga*, both of which are usually comparatively empty.

Back on the 710 to Fornells, duly refreshed, you are now very likely to be feeling the first pangs of hunger. To appease these a place worth recommending for a possible stop is *Sa Barranca d'es Carboner* at km 17, shortly before the turnoff to Arenal d'en Castell. This convivial restaurant offers local fare, especially lamb and fish, at moderate prices *(category 2)*, plus a lovely terrace and friendly service.

If, on the other hand, the idea of a *caldereta de langostes* – to be authentic it has to be in an earthenware dish – sets your mouth watering, you should keep your hunger at bay until you get to *Fornells*. There, right on the edge of the saltwater lagoon, with the reflections of the fishing boats mirrored in its still waters, you will find the *Es Pla* located on the causeway *(category 1*, lunch menu). This is in a little hamlet of some 300 souls which you should try and find the time to have a look at in any case. To round off your visit stop for a coffee in the *La Palma* bar or in the *S'Algaret*.

If the sun is still high in the heavens it is worth taking a sidetrip from Fornells to what was the old Roman port at *Sa Nitja*. To get there first head towards Es Mercadal and after about a third

of the way follow the sign on the right to "Faro de Cavallería". A relatively new road leads straight to the *Cap de Cavallería* on the north coast, passing the houses of Santa Teresa (on the right) and Sa Nitja (on the left). You can park the car at the barrier. From here make your way down to the cove on foot. The Roman settlement, where they have discovered several storehouses, a cemetery and the remains of other buildings since excavations began in 1979, is already impressive enough, but so is the silence and the feeling that the place itself is under a spell of its own. In the 2nd century A.D. *Sanicera* was still listed as being one of the three large towns on the island, but four centuries later every trace of it had vanished from the records.

Back on the road to Es Mercadal again, the almost steppe-like hilly ridges of the north coast are soon being replaced by pine woods which then give way to the lush pastures in the middle of the island. On the eastern outskirts of Es Mercadal a narrow asphalt road leads up to the rocky outcrop of *Monte Tòro*. After a few hairpin bends you will find yourself, at 357 m, here on the "roof of Menorca", with a fantastic panoramic view in all directions. On a clear day you can see the broad bay of Fornells glistening like a mirror to the north; all of this – except for the district around Son Parc – is a nature conservation area. And so is most of the green undulating countryside to the west. To the south you can pick out from the background the darker outlines of the *barrancs*, the fertile gullies that have been carved out of the soft limestone by centuries of rainfall. And beyond that sea and sky seem to blur and merge in the distance. You can make out Alaior in the south-east while, looking eastwards, there are the now familiar features of Albufera d'Es Grau and Cap de Favàritx. Again, most of the country in between has, since 1992, also enjoyed the protected status of areas of nature conservation.

After returning to Es Mercadal it then only takes about 30 minutes by road to get back to Mahón again.

② GODS, GRAVES AND HISTORY

 A spin through Menorca's thousands of years of history, fast-forwarding from prehistoric tombs to medieval ramparts. 1 day, about 80 km

The day out begins in *Ciutadella*. Fortify yourself first, though, by stopping for breakfast in, say, the *Café Balear* at the landward end of the port, or in the *Cercle Artistic* on the northern side of the Plaça d'es Born. And now, time to hit the road.

You will soon come across well preserved traces of long-gone civilizations just outside Ciutadella. Take the C-721 in the direction of Mahón and after no more than 4 km you will see a sign for "Nau d'es Tudons" on the right. Turn off here and after 1 km park on the large square. You will then find you are right in front of the famous *nau* ("ship"), so-called because what you are looking at resembles an upturned boat. This quite strikingly simple stone "keel" is one of the very earliest examples of man's skill as a builder and is probably the oldest existing roofed building anywhere in Europe.

Back on the main road carry on in the direction of Ferrerías. About 3 km before the town (km 31.6) turn left at the sign "Camí Els Alocs" (Binisues). After 3 km you come to an abandoned country school hostel. This marks the start of the track up to the *Castell de Santa Agueda* (alt. 260 m); it is quite hard going, and the climb can take 30–60 minutes. You can see what the fortress looked like over 500 years ago from the model in the military museum in Es Castell. But *Mons Jovis* (Mount Jove), as it was known in classical times, provided the island with its defence long before that, first under the Romans and then under the Moors. After centuries of obscurity it first cropped up again in records from the time of the Christian reconquest, when Alfonso III noted that the summit of one of the few high points on the island would be ideally suited for a fortress. As a consequence they built a small castle here, together with a chapel. This often also served as a refuge for the people living in the surrounding farms when they were under attack by pirates. It was not until the 17th and 18th centuries, by which time the rules of warfare had radically changed, that the fortress lost its strategic significance and fell into decay. This may also have been helped along by the legend that a magical golden calf (*vedell d'or*) was buried on the hilltop. Generations of adventurous Menorcans have since set about searching for the treasure with spars and pickaxes – and even dynamite at a later stage – but as yet without any success. What can be seen on the site are the ruins of the medieval ramparts. To make up for the exertions of the climb you also have a wonderful panoramic view over the island and out to sea from the top.

And if all this has given you an appetite then there is an opportunity to put this right close at hand. On the drive back to the main road a side road will take you to the *Binisues* restaurant *(category 2)*. There you will be catered for, in every sense, by an exhibition of antiques and traditional farming tools, a superb setting, and a good fish menu (freshly caught that day).

If you now feel like taking a bit of a break from the island's history, perhaps a spot of relaxation on the lovely coast would be a good idea. To this end take the PM-714 near to Ferreríes and head south in the direction of *Cala Galdana*. When you get there follow the sign on the roundabout to "Mirador de Sa Punta" and this will then take you to two places where you have a magnificent view over this lovely bay, which, despite all the development, is still stunningly beautiful. Families should head for the *Cala Mitjana* (about 2 km back, right, signposted, a charge for parking), which is easy to get to. If you are on your own, you can walk to the *Cala Macarella* (footpath on the west side of the bay from *Audatx* Hotel, a steep climb to start with, then the track widens out, around 2 km to the first sight of the bay). It will be well worth it!

The next side trip takes in the second of the three great periods of Menorcan history, the time of the *taules* and the *talaiots*. The historian Waldemar Fenn believes that the *taula* precincts represented a stone

clock that mark the passing of the seasons. Every settlement of any size had a feature of this kind, including the mightiest of all the prehistoric towns on the Balearics, nowadays known as *Torre d'en Gaumés*. You get there via Ferreríes and Alaior, where, shortly before entering the town, you turn right in the direction of Son Bou. After a good 2.5 km turn left, drive for another 1.5 km and you are there. This is a prehistoric town which is supposed to have been settled 5000 years ago and which reached its cultural heyday some time after 1300 B.C. when it was also at its largest and covered an area of more than 62,000 sq m. The population at that time would have been about 500. Then came the Romans, who were here in 123 B.C.. Although parts of the town were inhabited until the Middle Ages it had long since lost its former importance. The site is easy to get around but it is difficult to see it all, so you need to take some time to explore the whole complex. The best view is from the hill of the *talaiots*. The horizontal slab from the top of the *taula* in the temple precinct is missing and it may have been misappropriated – by the Romans perhaps – for use in a tomb. This seems to be borne out by a bronze statuette that was found, hidden in a wall, during the excavations in 1974. This is thought to represent Imhotep, the Egyptian god associated with medicine.

Once back in Ciutadella if you get the opportunity you can improve your knowledge of Menorca's history by visiting the *Museu Municipal (C/.Portal de Sa Font)* and the *Museu Diocesà (C/. Seminari)*.

Practical information

This chapter lists all the essential addresses and information you need for your holiday in Menorca

AMERICAN & BRITISH USAGE

Marco Polo travel guides are written in British English. In North America certain terms and usages deviate from British usage. Some of the more frequently encountered examples are (American given first):

baggage = luggage; cab = taxi; car rental = car hire; drugstore = chemist; fall = autumn; first floor == ground floor; freeway/highway = motorway; gas(oline) = petrol; railroad = railway; restroom = toilet/lavatory; streetcar = tram; subway = underground/tube; toll-free numbers = freephone numbers; trailer = caravan; trunk = boot (of a car); vacation = holiday; wait staff = waiter/waitress; zip code = post code

BANKS & MONEY

Banks *(bancos)*, savings banks *(cajas de ahorro)* and exchange offices *(cambio)* are better for changing money than hotels and shops. You get the best rates with Eurocheques (up to Ptas 25,000, make them out in pesetas). Banks and savings banks are normally only open from 9 am to 1 pm. Exchange offices in the tourist resorts are often open in the after-

Cruise ship and fishermen with their nets in Mahón harbour

noon as well. There are also cash points that can be used outside banking hours, and these accept all the major credit cards associated with Visa, Mastercard, American Express, Eurocheque, etc.

BUSES

Most tour operators have their own travel arrangements – at least during the season – for the journey from the airport to their holiday accommodation. Public transport is provided by three main operators: *TMSA, Tel. 971 36 03 61, Roca, Tel. 971 37 66 21 and Torres, Tel. 971 38 45 11.*

CAMPING

The decision as to whether to allow camping or not is up to the particular local authority or the individual landowner. Camping without permission is definitely inadvisable, and in nature conservation areas it is actually forbidden. There are two official campsites: *S'Atalaia,* 3 km from the the coast, in pinewoods between Ferreríes and Cala Galdana *(km 4 on the country road, Tel. 971 37 42 32, open April–Oct)* and Son Bou *(Ctra. Sant Jaume, km 3.5, Tel. 971 37 26 05, open April–Oct),* which is fairly new and has lots of sports facilities.

CAR RENTAL

You can rent cars, motorbikes and, in some cases, bicycles in all the large tourist resorts, in Mahón and Ciutadella, and at the airport. It is worth comparing prices; some companies advertise that costs are included, but this only covers depreciation and insurance. The rental firms at the airport tend to be the most expensive. Whatever you do, never leave any valuables, important papers, etc. in a parked hire car, not even out of sight in the trunk.

CHILDREN

Menorca is a child-friendly island and although it has relatively few major attractions to offer besides sea and sand it makes up for this in many ways with the good service it provides for families with children. Thus, for example, many of the larger hotels and restaurants cater specially for children. And in some places there are also special childcare facilities so that parents can enjoy a couple of hours of holiday time all to themselves.

CHURCH SERVICES

The local church services are usually in the Menorcan language as opposed to standard Spanish, which is less common. As an alternative, though, there are three Anglican churches on the island. These are in *Mahón (Camí de l'Ángel, 20)* and *Es Castell (C/. Stuart, 20* and *C/. Gran, 78).*

COMPLAINTS

Any business connected with tourism – hotels, restaurants, etc. – must by law keep a supply of the multilingual official complaint forms. These are also available in all the tourist information offices *(Oficinas de Información turística)*, and the tourist authorities take complaints very seriously if they relate to accommodation, eating out or any other service provided by the tourist industry. If there is any indication that these require some kind of action to be taken this will be dealt with in the *Fomento de Turismo*, so be sure to give the exact time and place.

CUSTOMS

Passport controls do not apply to visitors from countries that are signatories to the Schengen Agreement. On the other hand, visitors from the United Kingdom and most other countries simply need to have a valid passport. Citizens of the European Union (EU) are subject to the usual customs requirements and duty-free allowances. This means that, for your own consumption, you are allowed to import and export to and from Spain the following amounts free of duty: 800 cigarettes, 400 cigarillos, 200 cigars, 1 kg tobacco, 20 litres aperitifs, 90 litres wine (including a maximum 60 litres sparkling wine) and 110 litres beer.

DRIVING

Unless otherwise indicated, the *speed limits* are 50 km/h in built-up areas, 80 km/h on main roads and 100 km/h on dual carriageways or roads with hard shoulders at least 1.5 m wide. The *wearing of seat belts is compulsory* both in the front and the back seats (if fitted). The *blood alcohol limit* is 0.8, and spot-checks for drunk driving are becoming much more frequent.

A word of advice: the casual side of the Mediterranean temperament tends to show itself in the way the local drivers treat the rules of the road. This is particularly evident in their attitude to pedestrian crossings, which they largely ignore, and to traffic lights, which they are quite happy to hurtle through as the amber turns to red.

There are 11 filling stations on the island where you can fill up with super, diesel and unleaded *(sin plomo)*, or, as is getting to be more common, super or extra unleaded (98 octane). These are in Mahón (3), Ciutadella (3), Alaior (2), Sant Lluís, Es Mercadal, and on the road from Mahón to Fornells.

EMBASSIES & CONSULATES

British Vice-Consulate
SA Casa Nova
Cami de Biniatap 30
07720 Es Castell
Menorca
Tel: 971 36 33 73, Fax: 971 35 46 90

Canadian Embassy
Goya Building, 35 Nunez de Balboa
28001 Madrid,
Spain
Tel: 93 215 0704, Fax: 93 215 9117

United States Embassy
Serrano 75,
28006 Madrid
Spain

Tel: 91 587 2200, Fax: 91 587 2303

HEALTH

Pharmacies *(farmacias)* are marked by a green cross, usually in the form of a shield. Outside business hours the name and address of the nearest available chemist on 24-hour duty will be posted up in the window.

In the main holiday resorts there are Centros Médicos which specialize in dealing with holiday visitors. These are geared up to treating the most common tourist ailments and handling any language problems. UK citizens who can produce EU form E111 (this is available in the UK from post offices and must be acquired in advance) can also get free emergency treatment at social security and municipal hospitals. The Spanish for dentist is *dentista*. Before you go it is worth considering getting immunized against hepatitis A.

If you need to call an ambulance there is a 24-hour emergency number: *Tel. 061.*

INFORMATION

Spanish National Tourist Offices
In Great Britain
22–23 Manchester Square
London WIM 5AP
Tel: 0171 486 8077, brochure requests: 0891 669 920

In Canada
2 Bloor Street West, 34th floor
Toronto
Ont. M4W 3E2
Tel: 416 961 31 31, Fax: 416 961 19 92

In the United States
666 Fifth Avenue

New York NY 10103
Tel: 212 264 88 22, Fax: 212 265 88 64

Information and hotel listings on Menorca

– Oficina de Información turística, Plaça de S'Esplanada, 40, Mahón, Tel. 0034/971 36 37 90
– Asociación Hotelera de Menorca, C/. Jos, María Quadrado, 28, Mahón, Tel. 0034/971 36 10 03, Fax 971 36 28 57, open Mon–Fri 9 am–1 pm and 4–8 pm

On-the-spot information can be had from the two tourist offices in *Mahón (see above, open all year)* and *Ciutadella (Plaça de la Catedral, Tel. 971 38 26 93, open May–Oct)*, and from a *mobile tourist information centre* which spends a day at a time in the main holiday resorts in the summer months. There is also a new touch-screen service which has been available since 1998. These three computer terminals – located in Mahón, Ciutadella and at the airport – will flash up the main local information about the various places, such as street maps, descriptions, and archaeological routes, when you touch the appropriate place on the screen.

NEWSPAPERS

On Menorca you can get all the main English-language newspapers and periodicals; in the main tourist areas some even go on sale the same day. There is also a local monthly paper in English which is published under the name of *Roqueta*.

NUDISM & GOING TOPLESS

Unlike the other Balearic islands Menorca does not have a specially designated nudist beach. Going topless is not a problem though, and is indulged in just about everywhere. And there are also many who manage to acquire an all-over tan in the quiet, secluded coves.

PASSPORTS & VISAS

Even if you no longer need to go through passport controls you will still need a passport in the event of police checks or for cashing traveller's cheques, etc.

PETS

Any dogs or cats that are brought in must have been vaccinated against rabies. It will often also be necessary to produce a veterinary certificate on entry. This is a standard international form giving the dates of vaccination, confirmation that the animal is in a generally good state of health, and proof of origin. Some hotels cater specially for pets; as a rule, though, they are not welcome in restaurants and stores, and they are banned from beaches.

POLICE

Spain has three different police forces. The Guardia Civil (green uniforms, green and white vehicles) deal with traffic, rural crime, and customs offences. The *Policía Municipal* (blue and white uniforms, helmets and vehicles with black and white checked stripes) come under the municipal authorities (Mahón and Ciutadella) and handle urban traffic, while the *Policía Nacional* (dark blue uniforms, blue and white vehicles) is the unit responsible for prosecuting crime in the urban areas.

POST

Mail from Menorca takes its time; if you are in a hurry it is better to use a private, albeit more expensive service (*UPS* or *SEUR*), or the similarly expensive express service, *Postal Express* (aka Datapost). The postage for letters (up to 20 g) and postcards to the rest of Europe is Ptas 70. Stamps can be bought at post offices and from tobacconists (these official "tabacs" are marked with the national colours); post offices are only open from 9 am to 1 pm. There are main post offices (which also cash giros and normally provide a fax service as well) in *Alaior, C/. Doctor Albiñana, 1, Tel. 971 37 19 71, Es Castell, Plaça de S'Esplanada, 4, Tel. 971 36 71 07, Ciutadella, Plaça d'es Born, 5, Tel. 971 38 00 81, and Mahón, C/. Bonaire, 15, Tel. 971 36 38 92.* The post office at Mahón *(C/. Bonaire, 15)* takes telegrams over the phone from *8 am to 9 pm* on *Tel. 971 36 38 95.*

TAXIS

You can get taxis even in the smaller places, mostly from a specially provided taxi rank (sign). If none are available on-the-spot try the taxi call centre: *Tel. 971 36 71 11.*

TELEPHONE

Telephone cards (*tarjeta telefónica*, for Ptas 1000 and 2000) are increasingly being used for telephone calls. They can be bought in official tobacconists (carrying signs in the Spanish national colours), kiosks and post offices. International calls can be made from any public telephone box marked *Internacional* and from *locutores públicos*. The latter have the advantage of only charging once the call has been made. You will need to have a sufficient supply ready of 25, 50, and 100 peseta coins. The Spanish cheap rate operates between 10 pm and 8 am on weekdays, from 2 pm on Saturdays and all day on Sundays and public holidays. Calls from the *locutores públicos* cost around 5 to 15 per cent more than the usual rate, while from hotels they can cost up to 75 per cent more. If in doubt get help from the telephone company: *Telefónica, Mahón, C/. Ramón y Cajal, Tel. 971 36 16 17.*

The *dialling code* for calls to Spain from abroad is *00 34* (Spain no longer has its own area dialling codes). From Menorca to Canada and the United States it is *00 1*, and to the United Kingdom *00 44*. This should be followed by the area code (without the initial 0), and then the subscriber's number. *Directory enquiries*: national *10 03*, international *025*.

TELEVISION

Almost all hotels with television have satellite TV (mostly Astra, occasionally Hispansat) which can receive broadcasts in English. There are also four Spanish channels which they get as a matter of course.

TIPPING

As a general rule, although a service charge is normally included in hotel and restaurant bills, room maids, waiters and porters expect 5–10 percent of the bill. Taxi drivers and guides on sightseeing tours also tend to expect a tip of around 10 per cent. Poor service, should be duly acknowledged by not giving a *propina*.

VOLTAGE

The voltage in most hotels and hostels is 220 volts but there are still a very few place with 125 volts. You can have problems with plugs for older installations; adapters are available in any electrical store.

WEIGHTS & MEASURES

1 cm	0.39 inch
1 m	1.09 yd (3.28 ft)
1 km	0.62 miles
1 sq m	1.20 sq yds
1 ha	2.47 acres
1 sq km	0.39 sq miles
1 g	0.035 ounces
1 kg	2.21 pounds
1 British ton	1016 kg
1 US ton	907 kg

1 litre is equivalent to 0.22 Imperial gallons and 0.26 US gallons

WEATHER IN MAHÓN
Monthly averages

Daytime temperatures in °C/°F

14/57 14/57 16/61 18/64 21/70 25/77 28/82 28/82 26/79 22/72 18/64 14/57

Night-time temperatures in °C/°F

7/45 7/45 9/48 11/52 13/55 17/63 20/68 20/68 19/66 15/59 11/52 9/48

Sunshine: hours per day

5 5 6 8 10 10 12 10 8 6 5 4

Rainfall: days per month

9 8 8 7 5 3 1 3 6 11 9 12

Water temperatures in °C/°F

14/57 13/55 14/57 14/57 17/63 20/68 23/73 25/77 23/73 21/70 18/64 15/59

| Jan | Feb | Mar | Apr | May | June | July | Aug | Sep | Oct | Nov | Dec |

Do's and don'ts

Crime may be negligible but there are other pitfalls you need to watch out for

Safe swimming

The sea in the south of Menorca is known for its strong currents and these can be particularly treacherous on the larger, more open beaches. So always keep an eye out for warning buoys and don't swim out too far from those beaches that do have them.

The north of the island can be dangerous if Menorca's strong north wind, the *tramunta*, is blowing. If it is, that should really be enough to put a stop to any swimming. Never go into the water if the red flag for danger is flying!

It also needs pointing out, in this connection, that the cool breeze which is everpresent on Menorca can be very deceptive and is responsible for much of the sunburn suffered by those who visit the island, most of whom tend to be fair-skinned. It can lull you into a false sense of security, so you would do much better to time yourself rather than use your own judgement. It is worth remembering that skin specialists recommend only sunbathing for 15 to 20 minutes at the most. Protective sunscreen is a must in any case, even when swimming.

Luggage

Although your car is not likely to be stolen on Menorca, the theft of its contents can be a possibility. So never leave anything in the vehicle; you cannot even be sure that things are safe when they are locked away out of sight in the trunk. And let the hotel safe take care of your smaller valuables and any important documents, apart from those you may need to keep with you, such as your passport and driving licence.

Hawkers

Suddenly they pop up on the beach: hawkers peddling an array of fruit and drinks. Their wares are highly unlikely to conform to any kind of official or hygienic standards, so just remember – buyer beware!

Time-sharing

Who would really want to have an eighth of an apartment at a relatively high price! But time and again these crafty salesmen manage to bring off that kind of deal. Often they offer certain bonuses and other inducements to get you hooked, but there is only one thing here that you can really be certain about: when it comes to making their spiel these trained high-pressure salesmen can easily pull the wool over the eyes of any ordinary punter. Never, ever, sign anything straightaway! If you are seriously interested then get some other quotes or go to an official (API approved) broker. A relatively new EU guideline also provides for the the right to withdraw from any time-sharing agreement within 10 days of signing, and this even applies if a down-payment has already been made. There have also been cases in the Balearics of the contract being tampered with even before it is signed – so before finally signing up be sure to check the copy against the original!

Private land

Not every Menorcan likes to see strangers wandering over his land. Occasionally they have even been known to brandish their shotguns (mercifully without dire results), but more often they just let the dogs loose. So if you want to go for a walk (and above all if you are looking for somewhere to camp off-site) do speak to the landowner first. If walking on an established route always remember to shut the gates behind you again when crossing private land.

Shopping trips

This is not like crossing the Channel to buy duty-free goods. This is about those free trips that end up in hyping the sales of all kinds of tat that back home you could often get for a fraction of the price. What the *manteros* (carpet sellers) are pushing on this kind of free outing are camelhair rugs, footwarmers, cooking pots, miracle baths and all sorts of other supposed bargains. First you potter around the country-side for a bit then, over the coffee and cakes, it's down to business. Here too you are seeing psychologically trained salesmen at work, and it is often much more difficult to say no to them than you might think at first. The best course is not to go at all, but if you do end up with that fabulous carpet remember that under European law you theoretically have seven days to cancel the deal.

Forest fires

Menorca, like the rest of Spain, keeps on having to deal with devastating forest fires in the summer, and not infrequently these are started deliberately or caused by people's carelessness. From May to October the danger to woodland is particularly high because the earth dries out and is actually baking hot. Strong winds can also fan the flames so that the fire spreads. So please, please: don't light a fire outdoors, don't carelessly discard any glowing cigarette ends, and don't leave any litter behind at the picnic site (pieces of broken glass are a particular danger). If you suspect there is a forest fire immediately call the police *(emergency number 091)* or, better still, the fire brigade *(bomberos). The numbers to ring are: Ciutadella area, Tel. 971 36 39 61; Mahón area, Tel. 971 38 07 87.*When giving the details it is vitally important to be as precise as you can about the actual place, so when you are looking for the nearest telephone you must note down what it says on any road signs, etc.

Road Atlas of Menorca

*Please refer to back cover for an overview
of this Road Atlas*

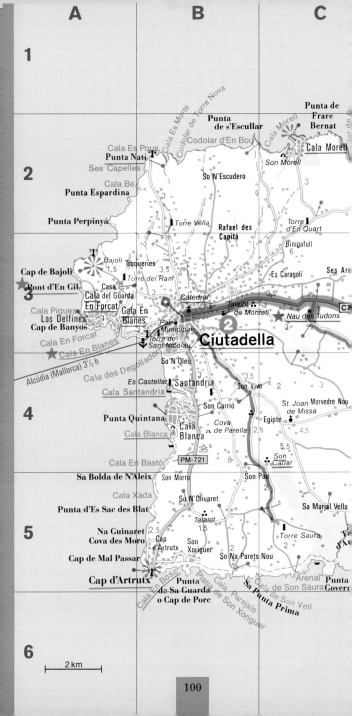

Grid columns: A, B, C
Grid rows: 1, 2, 3, 4, 5, 6

Cala Es Morts
Codolar de Torre Nova
Punta de s'Escullar
Codolar d'En Bou
Cala Morell
Punta de Frare Bernat
Cala Morell
Cala Es Pous
Punta Nati
Ses Capelles
Son Morell
3
So N'Escudero
Cala Be
Punta Espardina
9
Punta Perpinyà
Torre Vella
Rafael des Capità
Torre d'En Quart
Binigafull
6
Bajolí
1.5
Troqueries
3.5
Es Caragolí
Ses Are
Cap de Bajolí
Torre del Ram
3
Es Caragolí
Pont d'En Gil
Casa En Forcat
Catedral
3.5
Talaiot de Montefí
Nau des Tudons
C7
Cala Piques
Los Delfines
Cap de Banyos
1
Cala En Blanes
Pal. Municipal
Torre de Sant Nicolau
Ciutadella
3
Cala En Forcat
Cala En Blanes
So N'Oleo
Alcúdia (Mallorca) 3½ h
Cala des Degollador
3
3.5
Es Castellar
Santandria
Son Vivó
St. Joan de Missa
Morvedre Nou
Cala Santandria
2
Punta Quintana
Son Carrió
Egipte
4.5
Cala Blanca
Cala Blanca
Cova de Parella
2.5
5.5
Cala En Bastó
PM-721
8
Son Catlar
Sa Bolda de N'Aleix
Son Morro
Son Pau
2
Cala Xada
So N'Olivaret
Sa Marjal Vella
Punta d'Es Sac des Blat
Talaiot
1.5
Na Guinaret
Cova des Moro
2.5
Cap d'Artrutx
Son Xoriguer
So Na Parets Nou
2
Torre Saura
2
Cap de Mal Passar
Cap d'Artrutx
Punta de Sa Guarda o Cap de Porc
Cala En Bosc
Platja de Son Xoriguer
Cala Parejals
Arenal
Cala de Son Saura
Cala de Son Vell
Sa Punta Prima
Punta Goverr

2 km

100

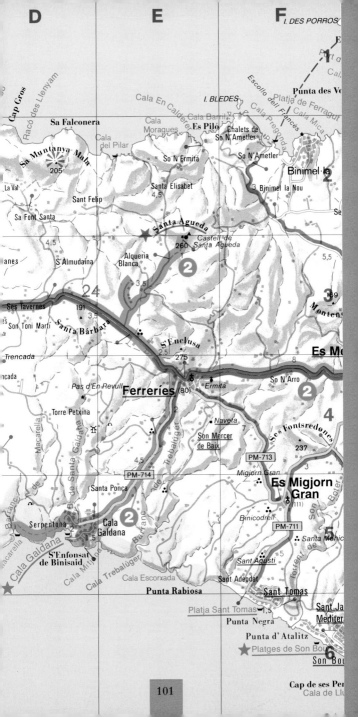

D   **E**   **F**   *I. DES PORROS*

1

I. BLEDES

Punta des Ve

Punta de Ferragu

Platja de Ferragu

Cala Pregonda

Cala En Caldera

Cap Gros

Racó des Llenyam

Sa Falconera

Cala Barril

Es Pilo

Cala Moragues

Chalets de So N'Ametler

So N'Ametler

Cala del Pilar

Sa Muntanya Mala

205

So N'Ermitá

Santa Elisabet
4,5

Binimel·la

Bjnimel la Nou

La Val

Sant Felip

Sa Font Santa

4,5

Santa Agueda

Castell de Santa Agueda
260

5,5

·anes

S'Almudaina

Alquería Blanca

2

3,5

169

Ses Tavernes

24

191

3,5

Montem

·es Son Toni Martí

a

Santa Bárbara

S'Enclusa
2.5
275

8

Es Me

Trencada

·ncada

Pas d'En Revull

Ferreries *(80)*

Ermita

So N'Arro

2

4

Torre Petxina

Naveta

Ses Fontsredones
237

Son Mercer de Baix

7

Macarella

de Santa Galdana

PM-713

4,5

Migjorn Gran

Es Migjorn Gran
(111)

PM-714

Santa Ponça

Barranc de Trebalúger

de

Binicodrell

PM-711

5

·e de

Barranc de

Serpentoña

2

Cala Galdana
1,5

Santa Mónica

5

Son Boter

Torrent

S'Enfonsat de Binisaid

Cala Mitjan

Sant Agustí

Cala Trebalúger

Cala Escorxada

Sant Adeodat

Punta Rabiosa

Platja Sant Tomas *1,5*

Sant Tomas

Sant Ja

Mediter

Punta Negra

Punta d'Atalitz

Platges de Son Bou

6

Son Bou

Cap de ses Per

Cala de Llu

101

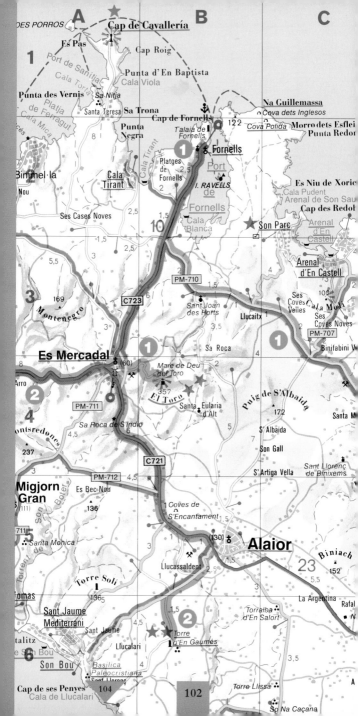

A

1

DES PORROS

Es Pas

Port de Sanitja

Cala Torta

Punta des Vernis · Sa Nitja

Platja de Ferragut

Santa Teresa · Sa Trona

Cala Mica

Punta Negra

Bimmel·la

Nou

Cala Tirant

Ses Cases Noves

2,5

2,5

1,5

5,5

3

169

Montenegro

3

Es Mercadal

(60)

8

Arro

2

4

237

ontsredones

3

Migjorn Gran

(111)

Es Bec Nou

136

711

Santa Monica

Torrent de

Boter

Sant Jaume Mediterrani

136

Sant Jaume

atalitz

e Son Bou

Son Bou

Basílica Paleocristiana

Sant Llorenç

Cap de ses Penyes

Cala de Llucalari

104

B

Cap de Cavallería

Cap Roig

Punta d'En Baptista

Cala Viola

Cap de Fornells

Talaia de Fornells

1

Fornells

Platges de Fornells

2,5

2

Port

I. RAVELLS de

Fornells

Cala Blanca

10

PM-710

C723

1,5

Sant Joan des Horts

3,5

1

Sa Roca

Mare de Deu del Toro

357

El Toro

Santa Eulària d'Alt

Sa Roca de S'Indio

4,5

C721

PM-711

PM-712 4,5

2

Coves de S'Encantament

1,5

1

3

1

(130)

Llucassaldent

1

Alaior

1,5

2,5

3

Torre Soli

1,5

2

Llucalari

Torre d'En Gaumés

4

Torre Llissa

102

C

Na Guillemassa

Cova dets Inglesos

122

Cova Polida

Morro dets Esfleí

Punta Redor

Es Niu de Xoric

Cala Pudent

Arenal de Son Sau

Cap des Redol

Arenal d'En Castell

Son Parc

2

Arenal d'En Castell

Ses Coves Velles

102

Cala Mol

Ses Coves Noves

PM-707

Llucaitx

4

1

Binifabini V

Puig de S'Albaida

172

Santa M

S'Albaida

7

Son Gall

Sant Llorenç de Binixems

S'Artiga Vella

23

Biniach

152

5,5

La Argentina

Rafal

Torralba d'En Salort

3,5

N

A

So Na Caçana